365 DAYS OF PLAY

Activities for Every Day of the Year

BY
MEGAN HEWES BUTLER

ILLUSTRATED BY
EMILY BALSLEY

Odd Dot • New York

FOR BEN + ELLINGTON + ORIN—
I LOVE YOU ALL THE TIME,
NO MATTER WHAT. —MHB

TO STEPHEN,
FOR ALL THE REMINDERS TO TAKE A BREAK
AND HAVE SOME FUN! —EB

Odd Dot
120 Broadway
New York, NY 10271
OddDot.com

Library of Congress Cataloging-in-Publication Data is available.

ISBN 978-1-250-75588-9

WRITER Megan Hewes Butler
ILLUSTRATOR Emily Balsley
DESIGNER Christina Quintero
EDITORS Nathalie Le Du & Justin Krasner

Our books may be purchased in bulk for promotional, educational, or business use.
Please contact your local bookseller or the Macmillan Corporate and Premium Sales Department
at (800) 221-7945 ext. 5442 or by email at MacmillanSpecialMarkets@macmillan.com.

Printed in China by 1010 Printing International Limited, Kwun Tong, Hong Kong

First edition, 2022

10 9 8 7 6 5 4 3 2 1

INTRODUCTION

Today is Day 1 of 365 days of play.

This book is your guide to the **ultimate year of play**. Rainy days, holidays, sick days, weekdays, leap days, game days, dog days, bad days, birthdays, and Fri-yays are all the right days—for play!

Create a game wherever you are and with whatever you have—swing a pendulum, launch a parachute, shoot a confetti cannon, or throw a boomerang. Tie a square knot or untangle a human knot. Make an egg you can float, bounce, or keep forever. Observe chemical reactions and capillary action, or even lower the freezing point of water to make . . . ice cream! Did I mention: Glow-in-the-dark messages? Worms you can eat? Or thaumatropes and kaleidoscopes?

Open this book to any page and get curious. Let's explore, learn, and make something new together. Let's play all day. Let's play every day.

I had a blast researching, experimenting, exploring (occasionally exploding), and figuring out new things while writing this book.

Yours in discovery, invention, and making lots of worthwhile messes as we go.

—MHB

HOW TO PLAY ALL DAY

Flip open this book to any page to get started. Keep an eye out for these icons:

SCIENCE EXPERIMENT

Eager to make things mix, grow, bubble, erupt, float, and change color? With these projects you'll learn why it looks like magic, but it's actually science!

Check out these projects if you like to taste-test, stir, pour, measure, whisk, and decorate—or if you're just hungry!

RECIPE

MAKE SOMETHING

If you like to turn paper, water, glue, and other items around your house into toys, art, games, slime, and more—these projects are for you.

Your creativity can turn mud into pies, secret words into your own spy language, and soap into fish. Check out these projects for more.

USE YOUR IMAGINATION

TIPS, TRICKS, AND PRANKS

Tips, tricks, and pranks says it all— wow your friends, amaze your parents, and learn skills you'll use for life (and laughs!).

THIS BOOK WILL SHOW YOU HOW TO:

FOLD A PAPER CUP

Sheet of paper

Scissors

① Cut a sheet of paper into a square:

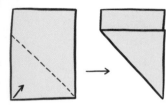

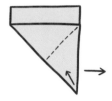

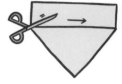

Fold up one lower corner of your paper until it matches the other side.

Fold up the other lower corner in the same way.

Cut off the top flap (you will not need this part), and unfold your square.

②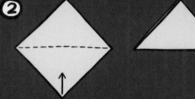

Fold your square sheet of paper in half diagonally.

③

Fold the left corner across the triangle so that it touches the other side. The line across the top of the folded corner should be straight.

④

Fold in the right corner across in the same way.

⑤  FLIP! **⑥**

Fold the top flap down. Then flip it over, and fold the other top flap down.

Open it up.

Fill your cup with water, and take a sip!

Fold another cup for your favorite snack.

BUILD A CONFETTI CANNON

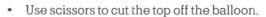

Scissors

Balloon

Toilet Paper Tube

Tape

Colored paper
(2 or more pieces)

- Use scissors to cut the top off the balloon.
- Stretch the balloon around one end of the toilet paper tube.
- Secure it with a piece of tape (or two) wrapped all the way around.
- Cut small shapes out of the colored paper to make a few handfuls of confetti. Pour it into the open side of the tube.

Let's party: Pull the balloon down as far as you can, and let it fly.

GROW STALACTITES AND STALAGMITES

Stalactites and stalagmites form when water seeps through rock. The water dissolves minerals or other substances in the rock, like limestone or calcium salts, and picks up small amounts. As the water drips, it leaves behind an "icicle," called a stalactite. As the water builds up on the floor, it forms a mound, called a stalagmite.

2 tall drinking glasses or jars

Spoon

Epsom salt

Baking pan

Piece of thick string or yarn about as long as your arm

Optional: food coloring

- Fill both glasses halfway with warm water.
- Add a spoonful of Epsom salt to both glasses, and stir to dissolve—it should be mixed in so that you no longer see it. Continue adding and stirring until some of the salts won't dissolve. (Optional: Add a few drops of food coloring here.)
- Place both glasses on the baking pan.
- Dip the string into the salty water until it is soaked. Then hang it between the glasses so that one end is in the water of each glass.

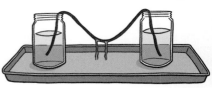

- Leave the experiment alone for several days, and watch what happens.

9

004 HOW TO
EAT WORMS

Box of chocolate
instant pudding

Mixing bowl

Whisk

2 cups of milk

4 graham crackers or
chocolate cookies (more if
the cookies are small)

Quart-size resealable
plastic bag

Rolling pin

Spoon

4 small bowls or cups (each
needs to hold about 1 cup)

4 gummy worms

- **Make the pudding:** Follow the instructions on the pudding box, using the mixing bowl, whisk, and milk.

- **Make the dirt:** Place the graham crackers or cookies in the plastic bag, and seal it. Gently roll over the bag with the rolling pin until the crackers or cookies are crushed and look like the texture of dirt.

- **Assemble:** Use the spoon to scoop about ½ cup of pudding into each bowl. Then add a scoop or two of "dirt."

- Top with the worms—then share and enjoy.

005 HOW TO
MAKE A FANCY MUD PIE

1 or more old containers:
baking pans, muffin tins,
plastic tubs, buckets,
or pots

Small stick

Dirt

Decorations: natural
items like rocks, leaves,
pinecones, flowers,
seeds, and more

- In a container, use your stick and hands to mix dirt and water in about equal amounts to make mud. (Add more water if your pie is too thick, or more dirt if your pie is too watery.)

- Decorate your creation with natural items— pinecones, helicopter seeds, flower stems, and more. Use items with different shapes and colors to make patterns and pictures.

MAKE A GUMMY WORM WIGGLE

Cutting board and knife
Gummy worm
2 drinking glasses
Baking soda
Small plate
White vinegar

- With the help of an adult, cut a gummy worm into four long, skinny worms.

- In one glass, mix 1 cup of water with 3 tablespoons of baking soda. Add the gummy worms, and let them soak for 15 minutes.
- Sprinkle a thin layer of dry baking soda in the center of the plate.
- Pull the worms out of the first glass, and roll them in the dry baking soda.
- Fill the other glass ¾ full with white vinegar.
- Drop the worms into the vinegar and watch them wiggle!

It looks like MAGIC, but it's actually SCIENCE!

Each gummy worm soaks in baking soda, which is a base. Then the worms are dunked into vinegar, which is an acid. When the acid and base touch, there is a chemical reaction—carbon dioxide gas bubbles form. Can you see them on the worms? These gas bubbles rise to the top and carry the worms with them. When the bubbles burst, the worms fall back down until more bubbles form.

007 HOW TO
MAKE A PIZZA ON SOMEONE'S BACK

Offer to make someone a pizza—and surprise them with a silly back rub!

First, knead the dough.

Next, roll it into a circle.

Then spread the sauce.

Sprinkle on some cheese.

Chop some toppings.

When it's cooked, slice it into pieces.

When you are done, ask if they can give you a pizza back rub in return.

008 HOW TO
MAKE PIZZA ROLLS

Can of crescent roll dough

Cutting board and knife

½ cup of pizza sauce or tomato sauce

Spoon

1 cup of shredded mozzarella cheese

Muffin tin

Nonstick cooking spray

Optional toppings: thin slices or small pieces of pepperoni, mushrooms, onions, peppers, olives, or anything you like

- With the help of an adult, preheat your oven to 350°F.

- Take the dough out of the can, and lay it flat on the cutting board. Use your fingers to smush and join the seams so that it is a solid rectangle.

- Add the sauce on top of the dough, and spread it out with the back of the spoon.

- Sprinkle with cheese. Add any other toppings that you like.

- Starting on the long side of the rectangle, roll the dough tightly into a long tube.

- With the help of an adult, cut the tube into 12 slices.

- Coat the muffin tin with nonstick spray, and place one slice into each cup, with the swirled side facing up.

- Bake for 16–20 minutes.

009 HOW TO
PLAY SARDINES

Did you know that sardines are small fish? You can buy them packed tightly together in tins. In this game, hide yourself by packing tight—like a sardine!

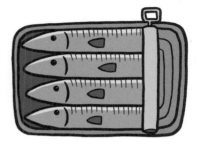

- Begin this game like hide-and-go-seek, but with a twist: Only *one* player is the hider. The rest of the players should cover their eyes and count to 20.

- Then the seeking begins. All the seekers sneak around to find the hidden player. When one seeker finds them they should quietly join the hiding spot so they both are hiding together. (But don't let any of the other seekers see!)

- The game continues until *all* the players are packed like sardines.

- To play again, the first seeker who found the hider becomes the new hider.

Play indoors! Play outdoors! Where can you pack the most sardines?

010 HOW TO
MAKE PARMESAN CRACKERS

Baking tray
Parchment paper
Spoon
Parmesan cheese

- With the help of an adult, preheat your oven to 400°F.
- Line the baking tray with parchment paper.
- Place one heaping spoonful of parmesan cheese onto the parchment paper. Repeat this until you have six piles of cheese. They should not touch one another.

- Bake for 4–6 minutes, or until the crackers are crisp and golden in color.
- Cool the crackers— then share and enjoy.

What do you call cheese that isn't yours? Nacho cheese!

011 HOW TO
MAKE GLOW-IN-THE-DARK SLIME

1 bottle of glow-in-the-dark glue (5 ounces)

Bowl

Spoon

½ teaspoon of baking soda

1 tablespoon of contact lens solution

Resealable plastic bag or tub

Optional: glitter, food coloring

- Squeeze the bottle of glue into the bowl.

- Pour in the baking soda. Mix it thoroughly with the spoon. Add optional items, like glitter or food coloring, now.

- Pour in the contact lens solution. Mix it thoroughly with the spoon. (It should get harder to stir as the mixture changes to a slime-like texture.)

- Pull the slime from the bowl, and knead it with your hands. Keep working with it until it is fully mixed, up to 1 minute.

- Hold your slime next to a light for a minute, then take it to a dark room or area to see its oozy glow!

- Store your slime in a sealed plastic bag or tub for 1–2 weeks.

Wash your hands after making and playing with slime.

012 HOW TO
WRITE A GLOW-IN-THE-DARK MESSAGE

Paper and pencil

Bottle of glow-in-the-dark glue

- Use your pencil to lightly draw on your paper. Outline the letters or pictures for your message.

- Use the glue to draw right on top of your pencil lines.

- Let it dry overnight.

- Hold your sign next to a light for a minute, then hang it where you want to see it at night.

013 HOW TO
SAY "I LOVE YOU" WITHOUT ANY WORDS

Use sign language to share a message without talking.

To say "I love you," hold your hand up like this:

This sign has the letters *I, L,* and *Y*—short for *I Love You!*

014 HOW TO
MAKE A MESSAGE IN A BOTTLE

Empty and clean recycled plastic bottle with a lid

Paper and markers

Optional: glitter, confetti, beads, or shells

- Peel the label off the bottle.
- Tear the edges of the paper so that it looks as though it has been on a long journey. Then write or draw your secret message.
- Roll your message up tightly, and push it into the bottle. (If you'd like, you could add some glitter, confetti, beads, or shells.) Put the lid on tight.
- Test it in the sink or bathtub.
- Give your secret message to someone.

015 HOW TO
MAKE CREEPY SPAGHETTI AND MEATBALLS

Turn a regular spaghetti and meatballs dinner into something your family won't forget.

Cooked spaghetti and meatballs

Cutting board and knife

Mozzarella ball (small works best)

Black olives

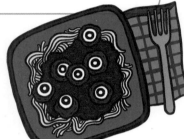

- Count the meatballs you'd like to turn into eyeballs.
- With the help of an adult, slice a ball of mozzarella cheese into thin, round slices. (If the ball is large, cut the slices into round shapes smaller than the meatballs.) You'll need one slice of cheese for each meatball.
- Cut each olive into thin, round slices. You'll need one slice for each meatball.
  - Assemble the eyeballs: Lay a slice of cheese and then a slice of olive on top of each meatball.
  - Add some extra sauce (blood) around your spaghetti noodles (guts) and it's time to eat.

016 HOW TO
MAKE DELICIOUS FAKE BLOOD

Teaspoon

Bowl

1 teaspoon of chocolate syrup

3 teaspoons of light corn syrup

Red food coloring

- Measure 1 teaspoon of water into the bowl. Add the chocolate syrup, light corn syrup, and 8–10 drops of red food coloring.
- Stir the fake blood.

Tastes great on ice cream, cake, and other desserts!

017   HOW TO

PLAY I BURY YOUR COWS

While riding in the car, collect (and protect!) the most cows while burying the cows that belong to other players (or turn them into hamburgers).

- The game begins by claiming cows: When you pass a farm, the first player to say "I see my 10 cows!" collects the cows. The player can say *any number* that they see or that they guess might be visible at the farm. However:

  - If there are fewer cows than the player guessed, the player collects 0.

  - If there are more cows than the player guessed, then another player can say "No—I see my 12 cows!" If this player is correct (and didn't overguess or underguess), then they collect the cows.

- Continue to collect cows as you drive. You must also protect your cows *and* eliminate other players' cows when you pass the following locations:

  - Cemetery: The first player to say "I bury your cows!" keeps their cows, while the rest of the players lose all theirs.

  - Church or place of worship: The first player to say "I marry my cows!" *doubles* their cows.

  - Hospital or doctor's office: The first player to say "Mad cow disease!" keeps their cows, while the rest of the players each lose half of theirs.

  - Fast-food restaurant: The first player to say "I cash in your cows!" keeps their cows, while the rest of the players each turn theirs into hamburgers. (And lose all of them.)

  - At the end of the drive, the player with the most livestock wins.

SEND MORSE CODE

Morse code is an alphabet code that uses dots and dashes to represent letters. A dot is a point and very quick. A dash is as long as three dots. The dots and dashes can be made with light (like from a flashlight or a lighthouse) or sound (like from a bike horn or staticky radio).

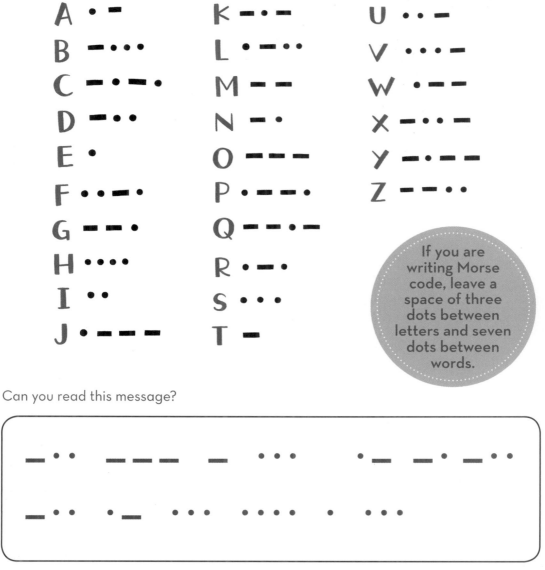

A • —   K — • —   U • • —
B — • • •   L • — • •   V • • • —
C — • — •   M — —   W • — —
D — • •   N — •   X — • • —
E •   O — — —   Y — • — —
F • • — •   P • — — •   Z — — • •
G — — •   Q — — • —
H • • • •   R • — •
I • •   S • • •
J • — — —   T —

If you are writing Morse code, leave a space of three dots between letters and seven dots between words.

Can you read this message?

— • •   — — —   — • • •   • — — • — • — •

— • •   • —   • • •   • • • •   •   • • •

Write your own message, and send it with a flashlight or whistle.

18

ANSWER: DOTS AND DASHES

PLAY ALL SPIES TO BASE

To win, move all your spies back to base without touching or crossing.

> Paper and pencil for each player

> Make up your own version, like: All Ships to the Harbor or All Astronauts to the Spaceship.

- Each player should draw a base in the middle of their paper—a shape with an open door. Then draw 15 numbered "spies" scattered around the base.

- Now it's time to play—trade papers. The goal is to get all the spies back to base—without *touching* or *crossing* any paths.

- Draw a line from spy #1 to the base. Then move to #2, then #3, and so on, in order.

- When both players are done, count any places where the lines touch or cross. These are each worth 1 point. The player with the least number of points wins.

TALK LIKE A SPY

Shhh! No time to make up a secret language? Talk to your friends like spies—but don't blow your cover.

BLOW YOUR COVER — let people know your secret identity

CHICKEN FEED — unimportant information given to confuse the enemy

DEAD DROP — secret place to leave a message for another person

MOLE — someone undercover for the enemy

INFILTRATION — secret movement of an agent into an area

POCKET LITTER — everyday things in a spy's pocket that help prove their fake identity (like a parking ticket or credit card)

BONA FIDES — proof of someone's identity

COBBLER — person who makes fake documents (like a passport) for spies

SANITIZE — remove secret information

19

COLLECT A SPIDERWEB

Spiderweb

Cornstarch

Sheet of dark-colored paper

Hair spray

- Find a spiderweb *without* a spider on it. Carefully search around for the spider. Gently tap the web to see if one appears. If no spider is around, continue to the next step.

- Put a small pile of cornstarch into your palm. Hold it in front of the web. Blow *gently* to cover the web in cornstarch.

- Work with a partner for the tricky part:

  - Have the first person hold the paper just behind the web.

  - Have the other person coat the web with hair spray (all the extra spray will go straight through the web and onto the paper). Take care not to spray your partner during this step.

  - Have the first person gently move the paper forward until the web is lying on the paper.

  - Both partners can use their fingers to carefully break any parts of the web still connected to trees, fences, or wherever you found it.

- When the web is connected only to the paper, check out your spiderweb art.

PLAY BEETLE

Be the first to draw an entire beetle.

1 die

Paper and pencil for
each player

Get creative:
What will your
beetle look like?
What other
animals can you
draw?

- The youngest player begins the game by rolling the die.
  Each number represents a part of the beetle:

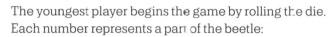

BODY   AN EYE

HEAD   AN ANTENNA

A LEG   A WING

- The player who rolled must draw the specified
  part of the beetle. However, no beetle parts can
  be free-floating—so the body must be drawn first.
  Similarly, the head must be drawn before the eyes
  or antennae can be added.

- If the player *can* draw a body part, they roll again. If
  the player *cannot* draw a body part (because it would
  be free-floating or because they have already drawn
  that body part), that player's turn is over.

- Players take turns in order of their age. The person
  who completes an entire beetle—with a body, a head,
  6 legs, 2 eyes, 2 antennae, and 2 wings—is the winner!

TIE A SQUARE KNOT

A square knot is great for tying a rope around an object, like a ribbon around a package, or for connecting two pieces of string.

2 pieces of rope, ribbon, or string

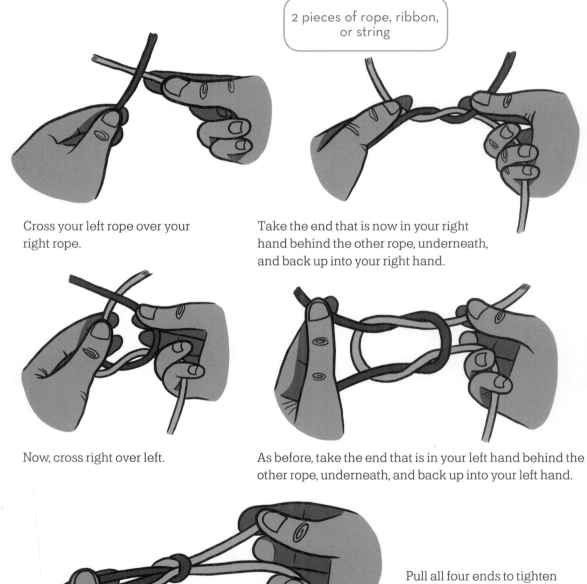

Cross your left rope over your right rope.

Take the end that is now in your right hand behind the other rope, underneath, and back up into your right hand.

Now, cross right over left.

As before, take the end that is in your left hand behind the other rope, underneath, and back up into your left hand.

Pull all four ends to tighten the knot.

UNTANGLE A HUMAN KNOT

Work as a team to untangle yourselves.

- Stand in a small circle facing one another.

- Each player should close their eyes, reach into the middle of the circle with both hands, and randomly grab two other hands with *each* of their hands.

- Hold tight, and open your eyes.

- See how quickly you can untangle your knot *without* letting go of any hands. Wiggle under, step over, and sneak through the knot to get untangled.

> The more players you have, the trickier it can be. Once you get the hang of it, try again with more players.

025 **HOW TO**

DECODE A BRAILLE CODE

Braille is a system of writing that uses patterns of raised dots for each letter of the alphabet. People who are visually impaired can learn to read these raised dots by feeling them with their fingertips. People who are not visually impaired can learn to read braille with their eyes.

A B C D E F G H I J K L M

N O P Q R S T U V W X Y Z

A cell with no raised dots is used as a space between words.

Can you decode this message?

> Write a message of your own!

026 HOW TO
MUMMIFY YOUR FRIENDS

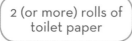

> 2 (or more) rolls of
> toilet paper

- Divide into two equal teams. On each team, pick one person to get wrapped up, just like a mummy.

- Give each team one roll of toilet paper. Have each mummy hold the end in their hand.

- When each team is standing next to their mummy and holding the rolls, say together, "Ready, set, mummy!"

- Each team should begin wrapping their mummy around and around with toilet paper as fast as they can. The mummy can stand still or spin if it helps their team. (But be careful, if the mummy moves *too* much, the toilet paper can break. If this happens, tuck the end into what is already wrapped and keep going.)

- A mummy is finished when you can no longer see any of the person's clothes or skin (except for space around the eyes, nose, and mouth). Whoever finishes their mummy first wins.

> Grab some buddies, and let's wrap some mummies!

027 HOW TO
PLAY BANDAGE TAG

Avoid being tagged to stay out of bandages—and out of the hospital!

- Select a large play area—outdoors works best. Choose a small space off to the side to serve as the hospital. Mark these areas with chalk, cones, sidewalks, or trees.

- When the game begins, every player can tag *and* be tagged.

- When a player is tagged, they must place one hand on that spot, like an elbow or leg. They can start running again, but their hand must stay in place—like a bandage.

- If the player is tagged a second time, they must place their *other* hand on the new spot. They can start running again, but both hands must stay in place—like two bandages.

- If the player is tagged a *third* time, they must go to the hospital and spin around five times—to remove all the bandages. Then they can return to the game.

- One player wins when they get *all* the other players wrapped up in two bandages each. (No one has any hands left to tag with!)

028 HOW TO
BUILD A TOILET PAPER MAZE

Roll of toilet paper or streamers

Painter's tape (or other tape that is safe for walls)

- Begin your course indoors or outdoors: Rip off a piece of toilet paper, and make a starting line on the ground.
- Continue to rip off pieces of any length, and create obstacles:
  - Make swirls on the ground that cannot be stepped on.
  - Make a path that must be walked through.
  - Hang toilet paper that must be stepped over or scooted under. (Wrap it around objects or use painter's tape.)
- End by making a finish line and navigating through your course.

029 HOW TO
BUILD A MARBLE MAZE

- Flip the shoebox lid over to the inside. Use a pencil to lightly draw a winding path from one top corner to one bottom corner. Take care not to cross over your own line.
- Cut the straws—some in half, some into thirds, and some into smaller pieces.
- Add glue to one piece of straw, and stick it inside the lid. Continue gluing more straws to form your maze. Make obstacles and false paths all over the lid, but don't touch or block your pencil path.
- Leave the maze flat to let the glue dry overnight.
- When it is dry, erase your pencil line.
- Place a marble at the top starting corner, and see if you can complete the maze.

Shoebox lid

Pencil

Scissors

Handful of paper straws

Glue (bottle or stick)

Marble, bouncy ball, small toy ball, or tightly rolled up ball of foil

HAVE A FROZEN FOSSIL DIG

Plastic bucket, tub, or container (the largest size that will fit in your freezer)

A few handfuls of small plastic toys (enough to almost fill your container)

Materials for digging: like a wooden spoon, a cup of salt, and a paintbrush

- With the help of an adult, clear a space in your freezer for the container. It must be able to sit upright—not tipped or on its side.

- Fill the container with your toys.

- Add water until it is a few inches from the top.

- Leave it in your freezer all day and overnight, or until it is frozen.

- Remove the container. Turn it upside down to pop or press the frozen water out, and place it somewhere that can get wet—outdoors or in a bathtub. Get adventurous using tools or water to dig for your "fossils."

031 HOW TO
MAKE CHOCOLATE ANIMAL CANDIES

- 1 box of brown sugar
- 8-by-8-inch baking pan
- Clean small plastic animal toys
- 2 cups of chocolate chips (or white chocolate chips)
- Microwave-safe bowl
- Spoon

- Pour the whole box of brown sugar into the baking pan, and pack it down very tightly into a smooth layer.
- Press your toys down into the sugar until each is about half submerged. Carefully lift each toy out of the sugar.
- Place the chocolate chips into the bowl, and microwave for 30 seconds on high. Stir.
- Repeat microwaving and stirring until the chocolate is melted. (This usually takes about 4 rounds, or 2 minutes. Stirring often will help prevent the chocolate from burning.)
- Use the spoon to fill each animal mold with melted chocolate.
- Place the pan in the refrigerator for 30 minutes or until the chocolate is hardened.
- Pull the chocolate candies out of the sugar—then share and enjoy.

032 HOW TO
MAKE A FOSSIL CAKE

- Box of chocolate cake mix
- Plate
- Chocolate frosting (see page 46)
- Butter knife
- White chocolate dinosaur candies (see above)
- 10–15 chocolate cookies
- Resealable plastic bag

- Follow the steps on the cake mix to bake a chocolate cake.
- When it has cooled, place it on a plate and frost it with chocolate frosting.
- Arrange your white chocolate dinosaur candies on top of the cake.
- Place the chocolate cookies into the plastic bag. Press the air out, and seal the bag tightly.
- Press down on the bag with your hands to break the cookies into crumbs.
- Dump the cookie crumbs onto the top of the cake, burying the fossils in "dirt."

033 HOW TO
DRAW HAND PUPPETS

> Washable markers

- Double-check that your markers are washable. (Very important step!)
- Look at the pictures for examples of different ways to fold your hand.
- Pick a spot on your hand to draw eyes. Then draw a mouth. (Add other features—a nose, antlers, ears, or rosy cheeks!)
- Move your fingers and hand to make the face move.

034 HOW TO
TRACE A HAND ANIMAL

> Sheet of paper
> Drawing tools (colored pencils/pens, markers, or crayons)

- Lay your hand down on the sheet of paper in any position.

- Trace it.
- Imagine: What does it look like?

- Draw the missing parts: eyes, legs, hair, tails, teeth, tiaras, or more.

DO A SECRET HANDSHAKE

Choose a combination of moves from below, or make up your own. Teach the combination to a friend. Do the moves together and you have a secret handshake!

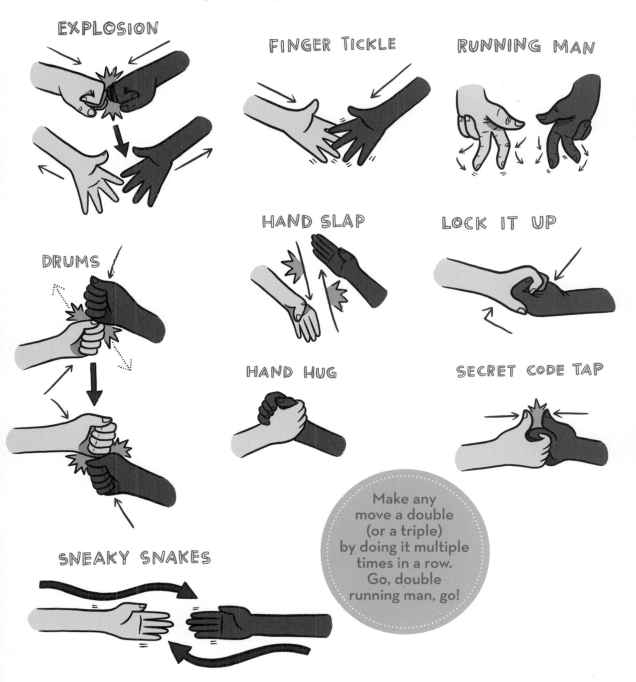

EXPLOSION

FINGER TICKLE

RUNNING MAN

DRUMS

HAND SLAP

LOCK IT UP

HAND HUG

SECRET CODE TAP

Make any move a double (or a triple) by doing it multiple times in a row. Go, double running man, go!

SNEAKY SNAKES

WRITE IN PIGPEN

To decode a pigpen code, write the alphabet across four special grids. Each letter is inside its own "pigpen"—some pigpens have only lines, and some have lines *and* dots.

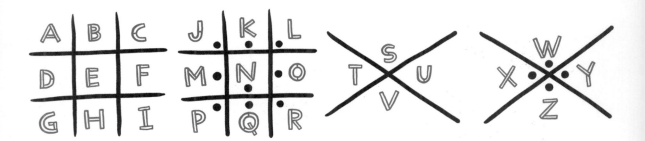

Use the lines and dots around each letter to figure out its symbol. Like this:

If you decode the entire alphabet, it will look like this:

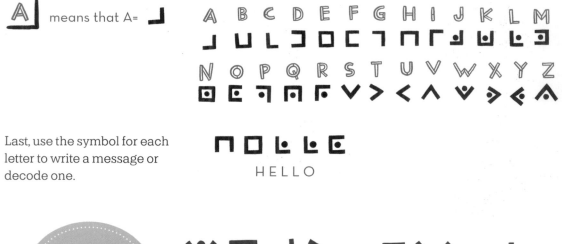

Last, use the symbol for each letter to write a message or decode one.

Can you decode this message? (Check out page 53!)

037 HOW TO
SPEAK PIG LATIN

Pig Latin is a secret language that's fun to speak. Pig Latin divides words into three groups:

For words that begin with vowels (A E I O U)	For words that begin with consonants	For words that begin with blended sounds
Add -*way* to the end	Move the consonant to the end and acd -*ay*	Move the blended sound to the end and add -*ay*
English: *apple* or *ice*	**English:** *zip* or *candy*	**English:** *smile* or *school*
Pig Latin: apple-*way* or ice-*way*	**Pig Latin:** *ip*zay or *andy*cay	**Pig Latin:** iles*may* or ools*chay*

There is a special rule for compound words: Simply split them apart, and treat them like two separate words. Pancake (pan-cake) becomes an*pay* ake*cay*.

038 HOW TO
PLAY GREEDY PIG

Roll your way to 50 points to win the game.

> 1 die
> Paper and pencil

- Roll the die. Whatever number you roll is your score.

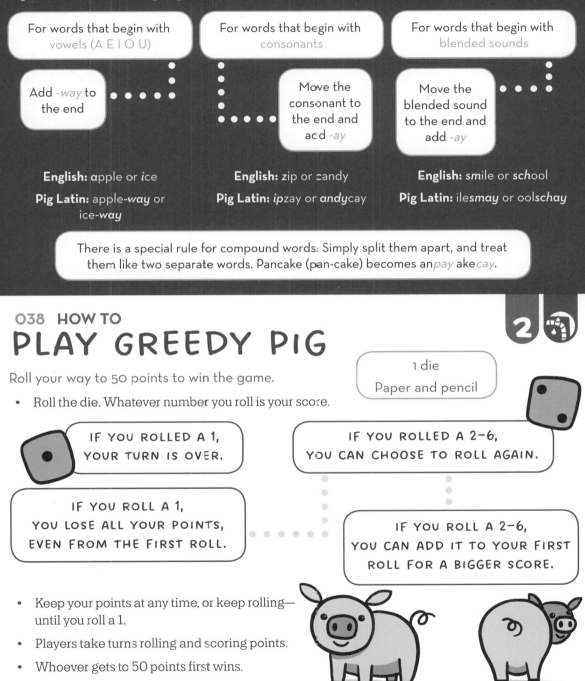

IF YOU ROLLED A 1, YOUR TURN IS OVER.

IF YOU ROLLED A 2–6, YOU CAN CHOOSE TO ROLL AGAIN.

IF YOU ROLL A 1, YOU LOSE ALL YOUR POINTS, EVEN FROM THE FIRST ROLL.

IF YOU ROLL A 2–6, YOU CAN ADD IT TO YOUR FIRST ROLL FOR A BIGGER SCORE.

- Keep your points at any time, or keep rolling— until you roll a 1.
- Players take turns rolling and scoring points.
- Whoever gets to 50 points first wins.

It looks like MAGIC, but it's actually SCIENCE!

In the first glass, the egg was denser than the water, so it sank. (The molecules in the egg were more tightly packed than those in the water.) But the second glass was filled with *salt* water. In fact, you added *enough* salt to your water to make the molecules more tightly packed than those in the egg, so it floated! What else can you float in salt water?

Did you notice the small bubbles that formed on the eggshell when you soaked the egg in vinegar? Vinegar is an acid. This acid reacts with the calcium carbonate in the eggshell to form carbon dioxide gas, so bubbles appear as the hard outer shell of the egg dissolves. Without its hard outer shell, the egg can bounce.

039 HOW TO
FLOAT AN EGG

> 2 clear drinking glasses
> 2 eggs
> Spoon
> Salt

- Fill both glasses about ⅔ of the way with water.

- Drop an egg into one of the glasses. Watch it sink.

- Add 3 heaping spoonfuls of salt to the other glass. Stir it until the salt dissolves and the water is clear.

- Drop the other egg into the salty water, and watch it magically float.

040 HOW TO
MAKE AN EGG BOUNCE

> Egg
> Tall drinking glass
> White vinegar
> Baking pan

- Carefully place the egg in the glass.

- Pour vinegar into the glass until the egg is covered. Wait 24 hours.

- There may be some residue from the eggshell in the glass—that's okay. Pour out the vinegar and residue. Take the squishy egg gently in your hand.

- Hold the egg 1 inch over the baking pan, and drop it. Then try 3 inches, then 5.

- How high can you go before it breaks?

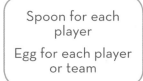

041 HOW TO
RUN AN EGG RACE

Win the race without touching or dropping the egg!

- Go outdoors and select starting and finish lines about 20 feet or so apart.

- Have all the players line up behind the starting line. Each should hold their spoon and place the egg on it. From here on out, NO ONE is allowed to touch their egg.

- Together count: "1, 2, 3, eggs!" While still holding your spoons, race for the finish. The first player to cross the line with their egg still in their spoon, wins!

> Spoon for each player
>
> Egg for each player or team

To level up:

- Add obstacles to run around or through.

- Skip, hop, or run backward.

- Make it a relay—each player must pass their egg to another player's spoon.

042 HOW TO
RUN A THREE-LEGGED RACE

- Go outdoors and select starting and finish lines for your race. They should be at least 20 feet apart.

- Have each player stand side by side with a partner. Use your bandannas to gently tie each player's inside ankle to their partner's inside ankle.

- Practice walking as three-legged teams: The two legs tied together must work as one.

- Have each team line up at the starting line. Together count: "1, 2, 3, go!" The first team across the finish line wins.

> Bandanna, large sock, or other strip of fabric for each team of 2

> If you master running *forward* three-legged, race *backward*!

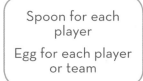

33

043 **HOW TO**
PLAY 20 QUESTIONS

Choose a partner and let's play.

- Pick a secret thing—anything. It could be a pet, something you are wearing, a favorite food, or a place you like to visit.

- Your partner now gets to ask 20 questions to see if they can guess your secret. But—you can only answer their questions by saying yes or no.

- If your partner guesses the secret in 20 or fewer questions— they win. If you keep the secret—you win.

Play again. Take turns picking a secret and asking questions.

044 HOW TO

PLAY ANIMAL, VEGETABLE, MINERAL

Choose a partner, and play this twist on 20 questions.

Pick a secret thing—anything. Tell your partner if it is an **animal**, **vegetable**, or **mineral**. You may have to be creative to decide.

A **GIRAFFE** IS AN ANIMAL. SO IS A FAVORITE UNDERWATER CARTOON CHARACTER AND YOUR NEIGHBOR. BUT WHAT ABOUT A HOT DOG? IT'S MADE FROM AN ANIMAL, SO YOU MIGHT CALL THAT AN ANIMAL, TOO.

A **CARROT** IS A VEGETABLE. SO IS THE TREE IN YOUR SCHOOLYARD AND A FLOWER. BUT WHAT ABOUT A WOODEN CHAIR? IT'S MADE FROM A PLANT, SO YOU MIGHT CALL THAT A VEGETABLE, TOO.

A **DIAMOND** IS A MINERAL. SO IS YOUR FORK AND A JEWELED NECKLACE. BUT WHAT ABOUT A PENNY? IT'S MADE FROM ZINC AND COPPER, SO YOU MIGHT CALL THAT A MINERAL, TOO.

- Your partner now gets to ask 20 questions to see if they can guess your secret object. But—you can only answer their questions by saying yes or no.

- If your partner guesses the secret object in 20 or fewer questions —they win. If you keep the object a secret—you win.

- Play again. Take turns picking the secret object and asking questions.

045 HOW TO
MAKE A PANCAKE BREAKFAST TACO

Eat tacos all day long!

Pancakes

Plate and silverware

Optional fillings:
Spreads like yogurt, jam, peanut butter, or maple syrup

Cut-up fruit like berries, bananas, peaches, or pineapple

Toppings like raisins, dried cranberries, or coconut flakes

- Place a pancake onto your plate.
- Add any spreads over your entire pancake.
- Place the fruit and toppings that you like in a line down the middle.
- Fold the pancake in half like a taco, and enjoy.

046 HOW TO
MAKE PANCAKE POPS

Make your regular pancakes *extra* special with craft sticks and dipping sauce.

2 cups of pancake batter

Nonstick skillet

1 teaspoon of butter

About 10 craft sticks

Spatula

- With the help of an adult, prepare your favorite pancake batter.
- Heat a skillet on the stove to medium, and melt 1 teaspoon of butter.
- Pour a few small globs of batter into the skillet to make a few small pancakes.
- Right away, place a craft stick in each pancake with a light press so that the batter covers it. The stick should go right in the middle, about ¾ of the way across the pancake.
- Flip the pancakes when they are lightly browned, and remove them from the pan when they are cooked through.
- Serve them with some jam or maple syrup for dipping.

047 HOW TO
MAKE PANCAKE EMOJIS

Good morning, smiley!

- Place a pancake on a plate.
- Place your toppings on the pancake to create a face

> Pancakes
> Plate

Optional toppings:

Fruit slices—bananas, apples, peaches, mangoes, or grapes

Berries—blueberries, raspberries, cherries, or sliced strawberries

Spreads—nut butter, regular butter, maple syrup, or jam

Treats—whipped cream or sprinkles

048 HOW TO
MAKE NO-BAKE YOGURT AND CEREAL BARS

> Small loaf pan
>
> Parchment paper
>
> 1 cup of Greek yogurt (plain or flavored)
>
> Spoon
>
> ¾ cup of cereal
>
> Knife
>
> Resealable plastic bag
>
> Optional: a small bit of honey, nuts, or dried fruit

- Line the loaf pan with parchment paper.
- Scoop the yogurt into the pan, and spread it out with a spoon. (Add any optional items now.)
- Pour the cereal on top of the yogurt, and press it in tightly with the spoon.
- Freeze for 4 or more hours. (Overnight works well, too.)
- Remove the pan from the freezer, and lift out the parchment paper.
- Let it sit at room temperature for 5–10 minutes. Then, with the help of an adult, cut the cereal and yogurt into four bars.
- Share and enjoy them right away, or wrap each bar in parchment paper, place it in a plastic bag, and store in the freezer for later. (Note: When the yogurt and cereal bar is frozen solid straight from the freezer, it needs to thaw for 5–10 minutes before enjoying.)

PLAY JACKS (WITHOUT JACKS)

> 10 small objects that fit in your hand at one time (stones, dried beans, small toy figures, etc.)
>
> Bouncy ball

Decide who goes first by *FLIPPING*:

- Hold all the objects in your palm.
- Quickly toss them up, and flip over your hand.
- Try to catch them *all* on the back of your hand.
- Whichever player catches the most (or any!) goes first.

The first player begins *ONESIES*:

- Toss all 10 objects onto the ground.
- Toss the ball into the air, and grab 1 object. Then grab the ball.
- The ball may bounce one time, but you must grab it before it bounces again.

**If you can't do that, it's the next player's turn.
Start a brand-new round of onesies on your next turn.**

If you win, keep going. Pick up all 10 objects in your hand, one at a time.

After *ONESIES*, start *TWOSIES*:

- Grab 2 objects at a time. Keep going, 2 at a time, until you have all 10.
- If you lose at twosies, start your next turn at twosies.

After *TWOSIES*, start *THREESIES*:

- Grab 3 objects at a time.
- On your last turn of threesies, pick up the 1 leftover jack.
- Going through each round until you can grab all 10 objects in ***tensies***.

**If you can't make it, keep practicing.
The player who grabs the highest number of objects wins.**

PLAY JACKS WITH A TWIST

Here are three other ways to play jacks:

SPEED DEMON

- Bounce your ball, and pick up 1 object.
- Put it back. Bounce again, and pick up 2.
- Keep going up to 10.
- Can you make it with no mistakes, in only 10 bounces?
- Who can make it up to 10 *and* back down to 1 first?

CRACK AN EGG

- Follow the same rules as regular jacks, beginning with onesies.

Here's the twist:
- Each time you pick up an object, you must knock it lightly on the ground (just like cracking an egg) before catching the ball.

CHERRY BASKET

- Follow the same rules as regular jacks, beginning with onesies.

Here's the twist:
- Each time you pick up an object, you must store it in your other hand (just like putting cherries in a basket) before catching the ball.

PLAY SIMON SAYS

Play this game indoors or outdoors. Listen closely to sneaky Simon, and only follow instructions that Simon says.

- Choose one player to be Simon. All the other players will be followers.
- Simon begins the game by saying, "Simon says: Hop like a flamingo!" while hopping on one leg like a flamingo. The followers must copy the move and hop on one leg.
- Simon continues giving instructions:

Simon says:
STOP HOPPING.

Simon says:
MOVE YOUR ARMS AS THOUGH YOU ARE PETTING AN OCTOPUS.

Simon says:
BOUNCE LIKE AN ASTRONAUT ON THE MOON.

- Then Simon goes in for the win: "Cry like a baby." If any of the players follow *this* instruction, they are out of the round! Simon did not start with "Simon says."
- The game continues until Simon has tricked all the followers out of the round—then a new Simon is picked.

**To make the game your own, pick your own name for Simon.
Play "Hannah says" or "Franklin says."**

2+

MAKE A BUTTERFLY FEEDER

Hole punch

Paper or plastic cup

Piece of string about
as tall as you

Scissors

New, unused kitchen
sponge

Pencil and colored paper

Tape

Butterfly food (see page 41)

- Use the hole punch to make two holes in the cup, one on either side of the top.

- Push one end of the string through each hole, and tie knots. The cup should now hang from the string.

- Flip the cup over. With the help of an adult, use the scissors to poke a small hole in the middle of the bottom of the cup.

- Cut a small piece of the sponge—a square about 1 inch.

- Put the small piece of sponge into the cup, and push the corner down through the hole. (Make the hole a bit larger if you need to. The sponge should remain larger than the hole, however, so that it doesn't fall out.)

- Use your pencil to draw five or more flower petal shapes on your colored paper, and cut them out.

- Tape the petals onto the bottom of the cup (but don't block the sponge).

- Hang your butterfly feeder high up, like in a tree, to keep ants from finding it.

- Fill your feeder with a small amount of butterfly food. It should be enough to soak the sponge and leave a little remaining in the bottom of the cup.

- Make sure to wash the inside of your butterfly feeder anytime it gets dirty, and at least every few days, to keep the food clean and mold-free.

Butterflies are attracted to colors like red, orange, yellow, and purple.

053 HOW TO
MAKE BUTTERFLY FOOD

2 tablespoons of sugar

Medium saucepan

Soy sauce

Jar with a lid

The soy sauce gives the butterflies just a little bit of salt—a necessary part of their diet, just as it is in yours!

- With the help of an adult, measure and pour 1¼ cups of water and the sugar into a medium saucepan.

- Place it on the stove over medium heat, and bring it to a simmer. Stir a few times as you wait for the sugar to dissolve—it should be mixed in so that you no longer see it.

- Stir in a few drops of soy sauce.

- Turn off the heat, and leave the pan to cool for 5–10 minutes.

- Pour a small amount of the cooled liquid into a butterfly feeder. Store any extra food in an airtight container in your refrigerator for up to 3 weeks.

054 HOW TO
BE A BUTTERFLY

- Sit on the floor. Bend both knees, and place the bottoms of your feet together.

- Keeping your feet on the floor, bring them as close to your body as you can.

- With your hands on your feet, gently flap your legs up and down like a butterfly.

MAKE A SUPERHERO CAPE

Scissors

Large or XL adult-size T-shirt

Optional: markers, glue, sequins

April 28 is National Superhero Day.

① With the help of an adult, cut the sleeves off the shirt.

② Cut straight up both sides, from the bottom hem into the armholes.

③ Open it all the way up. Cut around the front of the collar to remove the front part of the shirt, as shown. Decorate your cape with markers or sequins and glue.

DESIGN YOUR OWN COMIC

A comic is a story shown with pictures and words. The actions, scenes, and dialogue are drawn in different boxes. Use these ideas to get started creating your own.

Sheet of paper

Drawing tools (colored pencils/pens, markers, or crayons)

- Fold the top of a sheet of paper down in half, then open it back up. Fold it in half from right to left, then open it back up. You should have four boxes on your paper.

- In the top left box, write the title of your comic.

- Number the remaining boxes in order: 1, 2, 3.

- In box 1, use pictures to show what happens first in your story.

- In box 2, use pictures and words to show what happens in the middle, and in box 3, show the ending.

USE SPEECH BUBBLES TO ADD WHAT YOUR CHARACTERS ARE SAYING.

USE THOUGHT BUBBLES TO ADD WHAT YOUR CHARACTERS ARE THINKING.

Tape pages together to make longer comics!

MAKE SILLY MUSTACHE STRAWS

Sheet of tracing paper
(or white computer paper)

Pencil

Sheet of black or
brown paper

Scissors

2 or more paper straws

Tape

- Lay the tracing (or white) paper over the mustache templates below. Trace them, and cut them out.

- Lay the tracing-paper mustaches on top of the black or brown paper. Trace around them, and cut them out.

- Lay a mustache down flat, and place a straw in the middle—almost at the top of the straw.

- Tape the straw to the paper.

- Sip and smile.

FOLD YOUR OWN ENVELOPE

Square piece of paper (see page 8—any size will work)

Glue stick

Fold the paper in half to form a triangle. Unfold it, and fold it in half the other way. Unfold it to see a cross-shaped crease in the middle of the paper.

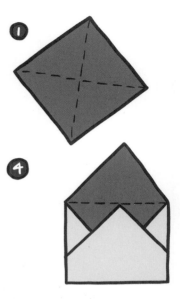

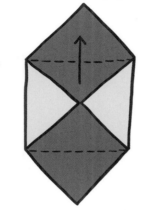

Fold in three corners so that they meet in the middle.

Unfold the top corner.

Fold the bottom corner up so that it touches the horizontal crease line near the top.

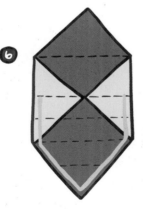

Fold the top point of this corner down so that the fold is even with the side flaps.

Unfold the bottom corner. Glue along the edges, where shown.

Fold in just the flap of the bottom triangle.

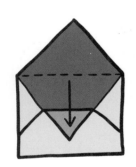

Fold up the rest of the bottom corner. Press on the glue to help it set and then let it dry.

Perfect for sending secret messages!

MAKE YOUR PUPILS SHRINK

> Mirror
> Flashlight

- Look in a mirror at your eyes wide open.
- Keep watching while you turn on a bright flashlight near your eyes.

Your eye has many parts:

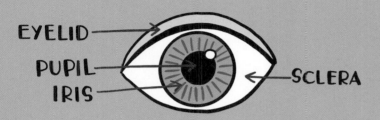

EYELID
PUPIL
IRIS
SCLERA

Your pupils are made up of tiny muscles that can expand or shrink. In a dark room, your pupils grow *larger* to allow more light in to help you see. Your pupils can also *shrink* when there is a lot of light so that less light enters your eyes.

PLAY SPOTLIGHT TAG

Play this game indoors or outdoors. You'll need a place and time where the light is dim enough to see where the flashlight is pointing. Avoid being caught by the flashlight to win!

> Flashlight

- Choose one player to be the searcher and hold the flashlight. The searcher counts to 10. The other player or players run off to hide.
- At the count of 10, the searcher begins the hunt: They can use the flashlight to find the players *and* to catch them. When the flashlight beam hits another player, the player is caught.
- The game continues until all the players are caught and then a new searcher is selected.

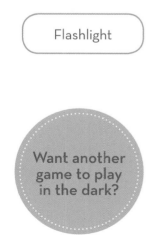

Want another game to play in the dark?

Shine the flashlight to the side, making a horizontal beam. Use this as a limbo bar to shimmy underneath. Lower the bar each time to make it challenging.
(See How to Limbo Dance on page 239.)

CELEBRATE YOUR HALF BIRTHDAY

Figure out when your half birthday is. Start with your birthday and then add 6 months.

- (For example, if your birthday is January 1, then on July 1 you are halfway to the next birthday. Or, if your birthday is September 22, your half birthday is March 22.)

Plan your celebration:

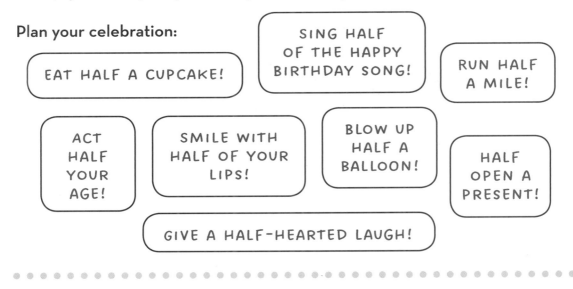

EAT HALF A CUPCAKE!

SING HALF OF THE HAPPY BIRTHDAY SONG!

RUN HALF A MILE!

ACT HALF YOUR AGE!

SMILE WITH HALF OF YOUR LIPS!

BLOW UP HALF A BALLOON!

HALF OPEN A PRESENT!

GIVE A HALF-HEARTED LAUGH!

062 HOW TO

MAKE BUTTERCREAM FROSTING

2 sticks room-temperature butter (1 cup)

Stand mixer (or electric beater and a mixing bowl)

4 cups powdered sugar

2 tablespoons milk or lemon juice

Optional: food coloring

- With the help of an adult, place the butter in the mixing bowl and beat until creamy.

- With the mixer on low, slowly add in the powdered sugar. Beat until creamy again.

- Pour in the milk or lemon juice, and continue to beat. (If the mixture is too thick, add another drop or two of liquid.)

- Mix in a few drops of food coloring if desired. Then it's time to frost. This recipe makes enough for 12 cupcakes or 1 small cake.

For flavors, mix in a few spoonfuls of cocoa powder or 1 large spoonful of nut or seed butter!

063 HOW TO
MAKE EASY PARTY DOUGH

Mix up this simple dough—make it plain or sparkly or scented. Then squish it, stack it, and form shapes, pictures, or characters. Or make playing pieces for tic-tac-toe!

> 2 cups of cornstarch
>
> ½ cup of hair conditioner or lotion
>
> Large bowl
>
> Resealable plastic bag
>
> Optional: glitter, sequins, essential oil, or small beads

- Pour the cornstarch and hair conditioner or lotion into the bowl, and mix with your hands.

- As you knead the dough, slowly pour in ½ cup of water.

- If the dough seems dry, add a few more tablespoons of water, and keep kneading until you have a soft ball. (This should not require more than 1 total cup of water.)

- Add in any optional textures. (Or divide the dough into three or four balls, and add different textures to each ball!)

- Store the dough in a tightly sealed plastic bag for up to 1 month. If the dough is firm the next time you use it, knead in a few drops of water.

064 HOW TO
WRAP A TRICK PRESENT

> Small present or note
>
> 3 empty boxes or containers: one small, one medium, and one large. (Each needs to fit inside the other, like a toilet paper tube, an empty tissue box, and a small cardboard shipping box.)
>
> 3 large pieces of paper: wrapping paper, newspaper, or old drawings and paintings you've made
>
> Scissors
>
> Tape

- Start by placing your present or note inside the smallest container (like a toilet paper tube).

- Use the smallest piece of paper to wrap it: Cut off any extra paper, and tape the edges closed.

- Now the joke begins: Place your wrapped present inside the medium container (like a tissue box). Use another piece of paper to wrap that.

- Last, place the double-wrapped present inside the largest container (like a cardboard shipping box). Use the largest piece of paper to wrap that, again! (If your paper isn't large enough, tape two or more pieces together.)

- Give your present to someone, and let the laughs begin.

065 HOW TO
MAKE MUD BRICKS

Mud (or dirt and water)

Ice cube tray

- Use your hands to pack mud tightly into each compartment of the ice cube tray. (If you do not have any mud, mix about 1 cup of dirt with ⅔ cup of water.)
- Leave the tray to dry in the sun for 2 or more hours.
- When the mud is dried, turn the tray upside down. Tap and press to remove the mud bricks. What can you build?

What could you use to form larger mud bricks?

066 HOW TO
MAKE SUMMER SNOWBALLS

1 cup of white hand lotion, body wash, or hair conditioner

1 cup of baking soda

¼ cup of water

Large bowl

Optional: glitter

- Add the ingredients to the bowl, and mix them with your hands.
- Once they are combined, knead them into a dough. If the dough still feels sticky, add a little more baking soda.
- Pop your bowl of snow dough into the refrigerator or freezer for about 10 minutes to make it cool, like real snow.
- Make snowballs or snowpeople, or shape it with cookie cutters.

Before you mix the ingredients, add a spoonful of glitter for sparkly snowballs.

HOST A WHEELBARROW RACE (WITHOUT A WHEELBARROW)

- Choose a starting and finish line about 20 feet apart.

- Each player should choose a partner and stand behind the starting line.

- One person in each pair should move to a push-up position on their hands and feet (or knees). (These players will become the wheelbarrows.) The other partner should pick up the wheelbarrow's ankles.

- When each team is in position, say together, "Ready, set, race!"

- Each wheelbarrow moves their hands, one in front of the other, while the other partner "drives" and carries their ankles toward the finish line.

- When the partners cross the finish line, change positions (so that the other partner has a chance to be the wheelbarrow) and race back to the starting line. Whichever team arrives at the line first wins!

Here are some twists:

Race the wheelbarrows . . . backward!

Set up some obstacles to race around (like balls or pinecones)!

Race up or down a hill!

Add some cargo on top of the wheelbarrows: Place a Frisbee or a leaf on the racer's back. If it falls off, that team must return to the starting line and try again.

Have each wheelbarrow wear a bandanna as a blindfold!

TELL A STORY WITH STONES

10 or more smooth stones

Paint and paintbrush
(acrylic and poster paint
both work well)

Permanent marker

Spray sealer

Making stones

- Wash and dry the stones.

- Use the paint to make a picture of a character, object, or place on each stone. Let the stones dry overnight.

- Use a permanent marker to add details—like eyes, hands, and clothing.

- With the help of an adult, follow the instructions on the spray sealer to protect the stones. Allow the sealer to dry.

Telling stories

- To tell a story, place all the stones facedown. Turn over two stones to start. Use your imagination to think of what could happen with those two pictures, and say it out loud.

- Turn over more stones to add more characters, objects, or places to your story.

FOLD AN ORIGAMI BOOKMARK

> Square piece of paper
> (see page 8—any size will work)
>
> Drawing tools (colored pencils/
> pens, markers, or crayons)

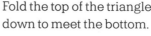

① Fold the paper in half.

② Fold one side of the triangle up to meet the top, then the other.

③ UNFOLD

Unfold both sides.

④ Fold the top of the triangle down to meet the bottom.

⑤

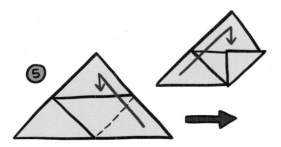

Fold in one side, and tuck it into the pocket. Last, fold in the other side, and tuck it into the pocket.

⑥

Decorate the top part of the pocket (this is the part you'll see in the corner of your page).

WRITE YOUR OWN POEM

An acrostic poem can be read more than one way. Not only can you read the poem regularly, from top to bottom—but the first letters of each line (or sometimes other letters) also spell their own word or message.

> Sheet of paper or notebook
>
> Writing tools (pencils, pens, markers, or crayons)

HARPER

ALWAYS SMILES

READS A BOOK EVERY DAY

PLAYS GAMES WITH HER FRIENDS

EATS LOTS OF ICE CREAM

REALLY LIKES TO LAUGH

- Write your name down the left-hand side of your paper, one letter on top of the other.

- Write your name again, using the first letter of your name to make the first line of your poem.

- For all the other letters of your name, write a word, a few words, or even a sentence that describes you or talks about something you like to do.

- Share your poem with someone you love. Then write a new poem with that person's name.

TWIST YOUR TONGUE

Tongue twisters are typically terribly tricky to try to tell.

IF A DOG CHEWS SHOES, WHOSE SHOES DOES HE CHOOSE?

NO NEED TO LIGHT A NIGHT-LIGHT ON A LIGHT NIGHT LIKE TONIGHT.

A BIG BUG BIT THE LITTLE BEETLE, BUT THE LITTLE BEETLE BIT THE BIG BUG BACK.

Make up your own tongue twister: Think of a silly sentence that tells a story. Choose words that start with the same sounds, end with the same sounds, rhyme—or all three!

USE NEW SILLY-SOUNDING WORDS

Ready to play a game? Memorize these silly-sounding (but real!) words. How many can you say before your friends or family members get suspicious?

CATTYWAMPUS
Means crooked, awkward, or going in the wrong direction.
"The pile of hot dogs is cattywampus."

TOMFOOLERY
Means silly or playful fooling around.
"I wish the dogs would stop that tomfoolery."

KERFUFFLE
Means a fussy argument or outburst.
"The dogs are having a kerfuffle."

DOODAD
Means a little object you can't remember the name of.
"What's that red doodad by the hot dogs?"

WOOZY
Means dizzy or not clearheaded.
"The smell of so many hot dogs is making me woozy."

SUPERFLUOUS
Means extra or too much of something.
"That's superfluous ketchup."

PLAY HAMBURGER CUPCAKES WITH SAUCE

- Work as a team to choose a silly phrase. Use one of these, or make up your own:

  HAMBURGER CUPCAKES WITH SAUCE

  SLIPPERY PONIES WITH NECKTIES

  GLOWING BEARS GO WILD AT DAWN

- Choose one player to be the questioner. The questioner goes around the circle, asking each player a question. Each player must answer the question by saying the silly phrase. For example:

  - WHAT'S YOUR FAVORITE FOOD?
    HAMBURGER CUPCAKES WITH SAUCE

  - IF YOU HAD ONE WISH, WHAT WOULD YOU WISH FOR?
    HAMBURGER CUPCAKES WITH SAUCE

  - WHAT DO YOU LOVE MORE THAN ME?
    HAMBURGER CUPCAKES WITH SAUCE

- The goal of the game is for players to answer the questions without smiling or laughing. When a player cracks, they become the questioner for a new round.

GROW SALT CRYSTALS

Epsom salt

Medium saucepan

Large spoon

12-inch piece of cotton string

Glass jar (that can be recycled)

Optional: food coloring

- With the help of an adult, place 2 cups of water and 2 cups of Epsom salt into the saucepan.

- On the stove, use high heat to bring the water-and-salt mixture almost to a boil. Stir until all the salt is dissolved—it should be mixed in so that you no longer see it. Then let the mixture cool on the stove for about 10 minutes.

- Tie a large knot at one end of the string. Tie the other end around the middle of the spoon.

- Lay the spoon across the top of the jar with the knot hanging down inside. The knot should hang near the bottom but not touch it.

- Pour the cooled water-and-salt mixture into the jar until the water almost touches the top.

- Check back in an hour, a few hours, and the next day. Lift your string out of the jar to see how your crystals have grown.

Add 5–10 drops of food coloring to the water-and-salt mixture once it's in the jar, and see what happens.

MAKE YOUR OWN ROCK CANDY

2 wooden dowels (about 1 foot long) or chopsticks

2¼ cups of sugar

Plate

Saucepan and large spoon

Glass jar with a wide-open top (about 2 cups—can be recycled)

Masking tape

Optional: food coloring, powdered juice mix

- Run the wooden dowels under water in the sink for about 30 seconds.

- Pour ¼ cup of sugar onto a plate. Roll the wet dowels in the sugar to get a starter coating.

- Pour 1 cup of warm water and 1 cup of sugar into the saucepan. Stir to combine.

- With the help of an adult, place the saucepan on the stove on medium-high heat.

- Add the remaining cup of sugar, and stir to combine. Bring the mixture to a low boil until it appears clear. This can take 10–15 minutes.

- Turn off the heat and leave the mixture alone to cool for 30 minutes.

Optional: To add flavor and color to your rock candy, stir in 1–2 teaspoons of powdered juice mix and a few drops of food coloring before the mixture cools.

- Pour the cooled mixture into the jar until it is about 1 inch from the top.

- Place one piece of masking tape across the top of the jar.

- Lower both dowels into the jar. Tip the sticky side of the tape up to hold the skewers. Place another piece of masking tape across the jar to hold them. (Adjust the dowels so that they do not touch the sides or bottom of the jar, or each other.)

- Wait. In 5–10 days you should see changes— sugar crystals will start to grow.

- When your rock candy is the size you want to eat, remove the tape and wiggle the dowels to free them from the jar, and enjoy!

076 HOW TO
PLAY GAMES WITH LEAVES

- Pick a partner or two.
- Take turns hiding something in the leaves, like a ball, toy, or even a large pinecone.
- See who can find it first or fastest.

- Divide into two teams.
- See who can make the biggest pile of leaves.
- Turn on some tunes, and have a leaf dance party.
- Scoop up some leaves, and throw them like confetti. See how many different colors or types of leaves you can find.

- Gather up a handful of your favorite leaves.
- Lay them out on the ground to make leaf animals.

077 HOW TO
MAKE A LEAF RUBBING

Flat natural materials (leaves—green or dried, pine needles, thin pieces of bark, flowers, or petals)

Sheet of paper (regular white computer paper or tracing paper works best)

Crayons or coloring pencils

- Lay a leaf (or other natural material) flat on a hard surface, like a table or book. Place the more textured side facing up.
- Lay a sheet of paper on top.
- Hold your crayon or colored pencil flat or at an angle, and gently rub back and forth.
- Experiment! Use different colors. Layer the leaves. Explore different natural materials. Use chalk or other art supplies.

078 HOW TO
MAKE COLORFUL LEAF PRINTS

Acrylic or poster paint

Small dish

Handful of leaves (they work best before they have turned brown)

Recycled scrap paper, newspaper, or magazine

Paintbrush

Paper

- Squeeze globs of a few colors of paint into the small dish.

- Place your first leaf (bumpy side up, showing the veins) on the scrap paper.

- Use your paintbrush to cover the leaf in many colors of paint. (Patterns and shapes work great!)

- Flip the leaf over, and press it into the scrap paper. Use your fingers to gently press all over the leaf. This helps to remove excess paint for a better print.

- Pick up the leaf, and press it onto your real paper. Use your fingers to gently press all over the leaf.

- Continue your design with more leaf prints: Repaint and use the same leaf again, change paint colors, or change leaves.

079 HOW TO
MAKE A NATURE MANDALA

Natural materials (like rocks, leaves, pinecones, acorns, flowers and petals, grasses, seeds, pieces of bark, feathers, shells, or small sticks)

Bucket, bag, or tray for collecting the natural materials

- Go outdoors and collect a small pile of natural materials—different colors, shapes, sizes, and textures—in your bucket.

- Choose one object to form the center of your mandala, and lay it on the ground.

- Make a small ring around the center object with another material or two.

- Continue moving outward with your circular design, adding one ring at a time.

Make nature mandalas in different seasons, and watch how they change.

MAKE A TOOTH FAIRY NECKLACE

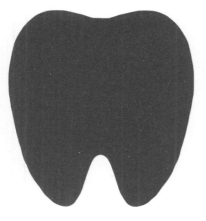

- Trace or draw this tooth shape on the sheet of paper.
- Cut it out. This is your template.
- Trace the tooth shape onto the piece of felt.
- Cut it out.

> Marker
>
> Sheet of paper
>
> Scissors
>
> Sheet of felt (about the same size as the paper)
>
> Fabric glue
>
> Piece of string or yarn (about as long as your arm)

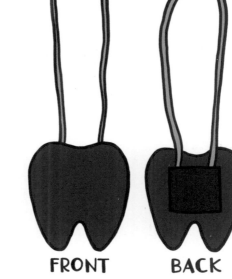

FRONT   **BACK**

- Cut out a square, smaller than the tooth, also from the piece of felt.
- Add glue to both sides and the bottom of the square. Leave the top open.

- Lay one end of the string down each side of the glue.
- Attach the square to the middle of the felt tooth, like a pocket, with the strings coming out the top.

- Let the glue dry overnight.
- Place your lost tooth in the pocket. Wear it like a necklace and then hang it by your bed at night. The tooth fairy might replace it with a surprise!

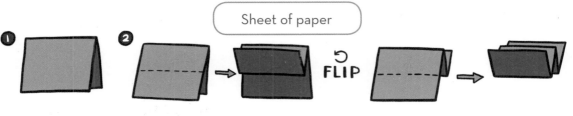

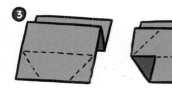

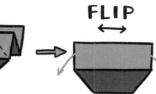

FOLD PAPER CHOMPING JAWS

Sheet of paper

① Fold the top of a sheet of paper down to fold it in half.

② Fold up the front side to meet the top fold. Flip it over, and fold up the back side. (The paper will now make a *W* shape from the side.)

③ Fold down one side. Take each bottom corner, and fold it up to the crease. Then take each top corner, and fold it down to the same crease.

④ Flip it over. Fold down the remaining side. Take each bottom corner, and fold it up to the crease.

⑤ Fold up both sides.

Flip the paper over, like a boat.

⑥ Fold the boat in half. Don't crease it—but, instead, pinch it near the top.

⑦ Open the boat up, and make a small tear, about a ½ inch, on the pinch mark in the middle. Fold down a flap on each side of the tear.

⑧ These folds should form long, thin triangles on each side. Then flip the boat over, and fold down two triangles on the other side of the tear.

⑨ Fold the boat in half to open up the jaws, and chomp away.

PLAY SUMMER SPLASH JUMP ROPE

Jump rope
Plastic cup
Plastic bowl

Gather your friends and materials and head outdoors. Dress to get wet!

- Choose two twirlers, who each take one end of the rope. Choose one jumper, who stands in the middle with the plastic cup half full of water.

- The twirlers start twirling, and the jumper starts jumping—with the cup. The jumper counts each dry jump, up to 5.

- Take turns being the jumper.

LEVEL UP:
FILL THE CUP WITH WATER. JUMP AGAIN!

LEVEL UP:
FILL THE BOWL HALFWAY WITH WATER. JUMP AGAIN!

LEVEL UP:
FILL THE BOWL ALL THE WAY WITH WATER. JUMP AGAIN!

What other containers can you use for water? A bucket? A Frisbee?

083 HOW TO
CATCH A RAINDROP

- Go outdoors on a rainy day.
- Look up at the sky.
- Open your mouth.
- Stick out your tongue and—if you are lucky—catch a raindrop. Grab a friend—who can catch the most?

MAKE RAINY DAY ART

Sheet of thick paper

Washable markers

- Draw a picture with washable markers.

- Take your art outdoors on a rainy day.

- Lay it down to get rained on for a few seconds to a few minutes.

- Watch what happens. When you like the effects of the rain, take your art back indoors to dry.

On a sunny day, take your art outdoors and spray it with a water bottle.

BUILD A RAIN PLAY SPRINKLER

Long nail

Empty and clean recycled 2-liter bottle

Duct tape

Hose

Loop the hose over a tree, chair, or swing set to lift the sprinkler up off the ground.

- With the help of an adult, use the nail to poke holes on all sides of the bottle—10–20 in all. (As you press with the nail, the bottle may flatten. This is okay—just pop it back into shape when you are done.)

- Take the bottle outdoors. Rip off a piece of duct tape about as long as your arm, and attach the bottle to the end of the hose tightly. (If one piece of tape is not enough, use more tape to seal it.)

- Turn on the water—it's sprinkler time!

CARVE A SLIPPERY FiSH

Baking pan | Spoon
Pencil | Paper clip
Bar of soap

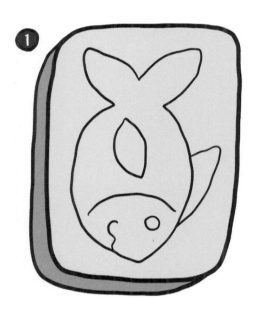

Work over the pan for easy cleanup. Use your pencil to draw the shape of your design on top of the bar of soap. You probably won't see the pencil marks, but you will make a light carving of the outline shape.

Use the spoon to scoop and carve away larger chunks of extra soap around the outside of your outline.

Use the paper clip to scoop and carve away smaller areas of extra soap.

Add finishing details to your design with the pencil.

087 HOW TO
MAKE SCRATCH ART

Thick sheet of art paper

Crayons

Black tempera paint

Small dish

Hand soap

Paintbrush

Scratching tools (a coin, fork, toothpick, or other small objects)

- Start by drawing on the paper with crayons. Add pictures, shapes, swirls, or just fields of colors. Cover all the paper.

- Place a few spoonfuls of black tempera paint in the dish. Add a small drop of hand soap, and mix with the paintbrush.

- Use the brush to cover your paper thickly with the black paint mixture.

- Let it dry overnight.

- Use the scratching tools to draw on the surface. Reveal colors underneath as you draw.

088 HOW TO
MAKE A TREASURE HUNT

2+

Treasure to hide

Writing and drawing tools

Small pieces of paper

- Choose a treasure, and hide it. Is it silly? Gross? Delicious? Hilarious? Hide your favorite joke in someone's shoe. Or a plastic bug in the arm of their coat.

- Go to where the hunt will begin. Plan where you want players to go next, and write a clue on a small piece of paper. For example, if you want players to go to your backpack, your clue could say: "Look in something I wear on my back." Leave the clue there, at the starting point.

- Go to your backpack. Plan where you want players to go next, and make a clue. It may be a picture of a toothbrush to lead them to the bathroom sink. Leave that clue there, with your backpack.

- Repeat this one or more times, depending on how long and tricky you want your hunt to be. The final clue you make should lead players to the treasure.

- Lead the players to the starting point with the first clue. Time to hunt!

FOLD A PAPER FOOTBALL

Sheet of paper

Drawing tools (colored pencils/pens, markers, or crayons)

1 Fold the paper into thirds the long way: Fold in one side first, then the other side on top of it.

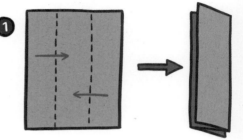

2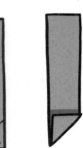

Fold up either bottom corner to line up with the other side. Crease it firmly.

3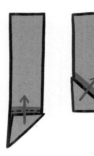

Fold this triangle up again. Then fold it up three more times until you are at the top.

All these creases should be firm.

4

Fold down the right top corner to touch the top of the triangle.

5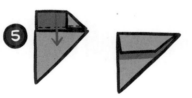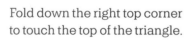

Fold the top flap down, and crease it.

6

Open the triangle, like an ice-cream cone, and push the flap inside.

7

Decorate and personalize your paper football with drawing tools.

Memorize these steps and you'll be able to fold and play paper football anywhere!

090 HOW TO
PLAY PAPER FOOTBALL

Use a paper football to score touchdowns and kick extra points.

> Paper football
> Coin

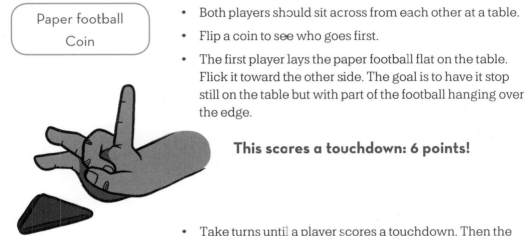

- Both players should sit across from each other at a table.

- Flip a coin to see who goes first.

- The first player lays the paper football flat on the table. Flick it toward the other side. The goal is to have it stop still on the table but with part of the football hanging over the edge.

  This scores a touchdown: 6 points!

- Take turns until a player scores a touchdown. Then the scoring player can kick for an extra point:

  - The defending player forms two L shapes with their hands and connects them to form goalposts.

  - The scoring player holds the football on its point. Then they flick it and aim at the goalposts. If the football goes through: 1 more point!

Check out How to Play Ddakji (page 173) for another folded-paper game.

- The game continues with the defending player. Both players take turns and try to get another touchdown.

- Play the game to 20 points.

MAKE A SHIRT FOR $1

Dollar bill

1

Fold a dollar bill in half the long way, making a tall rectangle. The back of the bill should be on the inside.

2

FLIP ↻

Unfold it. Fold each side in to meet in the middle at your crease line. Keep the back of the bill on the inside. The words *THE UNITED STATES OF AMERICA* should be on the left.

3

FLIP ↻

Flip the bill over. Fold down the white border at the top. This forms your collar.

4

Flip it over again. Fold in both top corners to the middle line.

5

Fold up from the bottom until you meet the *D* of *UNITED*.

6

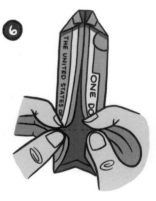

Open up the fold. Use both hands to pop out the two creases you just made.

7

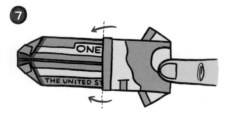

Wiggle the paper a bit as you refold the bottom back up to the *D*. The two popped-out creases will become the sleeves.

8

Fold the bill up again (from the *D*), and tuck it under the flaps of the shirt collar.

MAKE A PAIR OF PANTS FOR $1

Dollar bill

    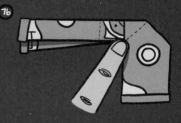

FLIP

Fold a dollar bill in half the long way, making a tall rectangle. The back of the bill should be on the inside. Unfold it. Fold in each short white end. Flip it over.

Fold in each side to meet in the middle at your crease line. Keep the back of the bill on the inside. Fold the top down to fold it in half.

Make some creases for the next step: Fold the top leg up toward the left to match the top edge. Fold it back down. Then fold it up toward the right to match the top edge. Fold it back down. Flip the pants over, and do the same thing to the other leg.

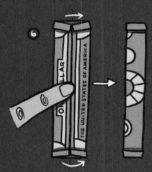 

Open the bill wide into a long rectangle (like in step 3). Fold the bill in half lengthwise.

Use the crease to fold up the bill by the center. Then fold the leg down. Do the same thing on the other side.

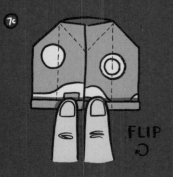

FLIP

Flip the pants over. Use both hands to fold one pant leg in half toward the center, into the hem of the pants. Then tuck the fold into the hem on the other side.

FOLD A PAPER WALLET

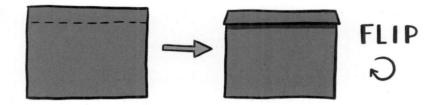

Sheet of paper

① 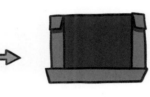 FLIP

Fold the long top side of a sheet of paper down, about 1 inch (or slightly more).

②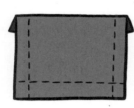

Flip the paper over. Fold in both sides, first each about 1 inch (or slightly more) and then fold up the bottom the same amount.

③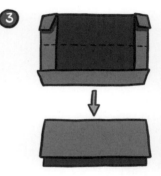

Fold the top down to the middle of the flap.

④

Unfold it, and fold it down again, tucking it inside each side flap.

⑤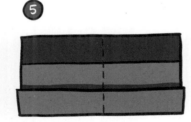

You should have two pockets running across the paper.

Fold it in half sideways so that these pockets are on the inside.

094 HOW TO
PLAY ODD BEANS

Win *all* the beans to win the game!

24 dried beans
2 small paper bags

- Have each player count 12 beans and place them in their bag.

- Begin by reaching into your bag and grabbing some beans. Secretly count them and then close your hand around them to hide them. Ask your partner: odds or evens?

- Your partner must guess if you have an odd or even number of beans in your hand.

IF YOUR PARTNER GUESSES CORRECTLY, THEY GET YOUR HANDFUL OF BEANS.

IF YOUR PARTNER GUESSES INCORRECTLY, THEY MUST REACH INTO THEIR BAG TO GIVE YOU THE NUMBER OF BEANS IN YOUR HAND.

- The game continues as you take turns reaching into your bags and guessing odds or evens.

- Whoever wins all the beans first wins the game.

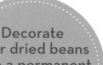

Decorate your dried beans with a permanent marker. Or play with jelly beans!

095 HOW TO
PLAY ODDS AND EVENS

Let's go again: Win *all* the beans to win the game!

10 dried beans

- To start, you will be Team Even and your partner will be Team Odd.

- Count together: '1, 2, 3, go!' On the word *go*, each player holds up either one or two fingers.

- Count all the fingers. If it equals an even number, you pick up a bean. If it equals an odd number, your partner picks up a bean.

- Whoever wins all the beans first wins the game.

Switch who is Team Even and Team Odd, and play again.

096 HOW TO
MAKE YOUR OWN FACE PAINT

Cornstarch

Lotion

2 small bowls

Vegetable oil

Paintbrush

Washable paint

Airtight container

- Measure 2 teaspoons of cornstarch and 2 teaspoons of lotion into one bowl. Add a drop of water and two drops of vegetable oil.

- Mix with the paintbrush until a thick, smooth paste is formed.

- Use the paintbrush to scoop about half the paste into the second bowl.

- Add a few drops (up to ¼ teaspoon) of a different color of washable paint into each bowl.

- Mix again with the paintbrush. If the mixture is too thick, add another drop of oil.

- Use the paintbrush to add designs to your face and hands. Wash off with water and soap when you are done. Store the extra face paint in an airtight container for up to 2 weeks.

097 HOW TO
PAINT YOUR TOAST

Milk (at least 4 tablespoons)

Muffin tin

Food coloring

1 or more clean paintbrushes (should be new and food-safe)

Sliced bread

- Pour 2 tablespoons of milk into two or more cups of the muffin tin.

- Add 2–4 drops of food coloring to each cup, and use the paintbrush to stir the milk paint. Mix to make your own colors.

- Then paint the sliced bread.

- With the help of an adult, put the bread into a toaster (or oven). Share and enjoy.

MAKE A PENDULUM PAINTING

A pendulum is a hanging object that can swing freely. Just add paint to make art.

Nail (or a kitchen skewer or chopstick)

Paper or plastic cup

Piece of string as tall as you are

2 chairs with open backs

Long pole (broomstick, rake, or long dowel)

Large sheets or a roll of paper (or smaller sheets taped together)

Recycled scrap paper, newspaper, or magazine

Tempera paint (or other liquid paint, like finger paint, poster paint, or liquid watercolors)

- With the help of an adult, use the nail to poke a hole in the middle of the bottom of the cup. Then poke two holes near the top, one on each side.

- Tie one end of the string through each of the top holes in the cup. Now the cup should be hanging on a loop of string.

- Set up two chairs, back-to-back, about 3 feet apart.

- Loop the cup on the string onto the middle of the pole. Then sit the pole between the backs of the two chairs. The cup should hang down but not touch the floor.

- Place the scrap paper directly underneath the cup. Place a sheet or the roll of paper on top of that.

- Test your pendulum: Pour ¼ cup or less of water into the cup. Swing it gently. Wherever the water goes, paint will go. Use extra scrap paper to protect any areas that may get wet.

- Pour ¼ cup or less of paint into the cup. Swing it gently. Push it into small circles, diagonals, or figure eights.

TIP: After your first color, use a different one to layer the colors on your paper.

TIP: If your paint is too thick, mix in a little bit of water.

PLAY CAR COUNTING

Count up to 20 together with your friends or family. Play anytime—even while riding in the car.

- The youngest player starts by saying the number 1 out loud.

- Then any player can go next by saying the number 2. This continues with 3, 4, 5, and higher—as high as you can go.

- Here are the twists:

> YOU CANNOT SAY TWO NUMBERS IN A ROW. YOU MUST TAKE TURNS.

> IF TWO PLAYERS SAY THE SAME NUMBER—THE GAME STARTS OVER AT 1.

If there is too long of a pause, more than 5 seconds, the game starts over at 1.

DRIVE TO 100

Here's another version of the car counting game to play with your friends and family.

- Each player in the game begins by searching out the car windows. Look for numbers on road signs, building signs, license plates, flags, or more.

- When someone sees the number 1, they say it out loud.

- Then any player can go next by seeing the number 2 and saying it out loud. This continues with 3, 4, 5, and higher—as high as you can go.

- Here are the twists:

> IF TWO PLAYERS SAY THE SAME NUMBER AT THE SAME TIME—THE GAME STARTS OVER AT 1.

> IF A PLAYER LOSES COUNT AND SAYS A NUMBER OUT OF ORDER—THE GAME STARTS OVER AT 1.

You can break numbers apart: For example, if you see the number 16, you could use it for a 1, 6, or 16.

- Count to 100 together to win!

PLAY TIC-TAC-TOE ON THE GO

Play tic-tac-toe on the go. The first player to get three in a row wins.

> 5 napkins
>
> 5 forks
>
> 5 spoons

Want to play in your kitchen or at a restaurant?

- Lay five napkins out in the pattern shown below.
- One player can use forks as playing pieces. The other can use spoons.

What else on *your* table could you use as playing pieces?

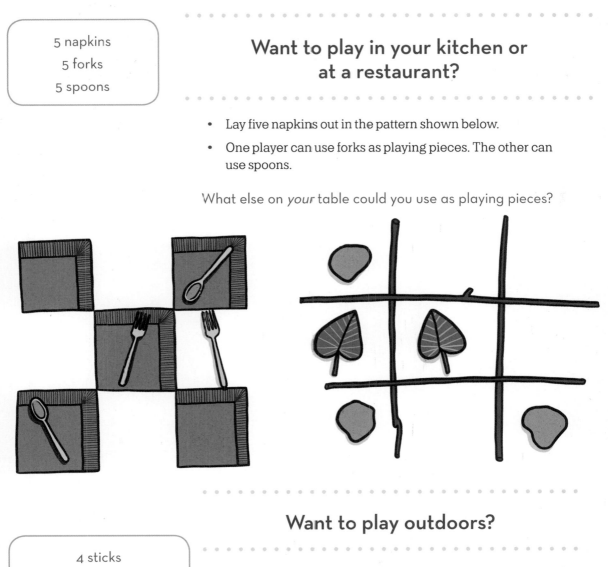

Want to play outdoors?

> 4 sticks
>
> 5 rocks
>
> 5 leaves

- Lay four sticks out in the pattern shown above.
- One player can use rocks as playing pieces. The other can use leaves.

What other things do *you* see that could be playing pieces?

MAKE THREE-INGREDIENT SLIME

4-ounce bottle of glue

2 bowls

Spoon

½ teaspoon of borax

Airtight container

Optional: glitter, food coloring

- Squeeze the bottle of glue into the first bowl.
- With the help of an adult, in the second bowl, use a spoon to mix ½ cup water with borax.

Note: If you want doughier slime, add up to 1 more teaspoon of borax. If you want slime that is runnier and gooier, use less borax (¼ teaspoon instead of the usual ½ teaspoon). But beware: Gooier slime can be a bit harder to clean up.

- Slowly pour the borax mixture into the glue. Stir with the spoon. Once it starts to come together (in 10–20 seconds), mix and knead it with your hands. Keep working until it is fully mixed, up to 1 minute.
- Store your slime in an airtight container for 1–2 weeks.

Add any optional items, like glitter or food coloring, while kneading.

A note about borax: borax is a mineral and a cleaning product. Only use it with the help of an adult. It is not safe to get near your face or eat. Make sure to wash your hands after making and playing with slime.

103 HOW TO
MAKE PUFFY SLIME

4-ounce bottle of glue

Food coloring

Bowl and spoon

2 cups of foaming shaving cream

3 or more tablespoons of contact lens solution (must have boric acid or sodium borate)

Airtight container

- Squeeze the bottle of glue into the bowl. Add a few drops of food coloring, and mix with a spoon.

- Add the shaving cream, and mix again with a spoon or your hands until it is fluffy.

- Add the contact lens solution a little bit at a time. Mix as you go. (If the slime is sticky, add a little more solution.)

- Store your slime in an airtight container for about a week.

104 HOW TO
MAKE YOUR OWN WINDOW CLINGS

Bottle of school glue

Dish soap

2 or more small dishes

Food coloring

Paintbrush

Gallon-size resealable plastic bag

- Place roughly 2 tablespoons of glue and 2 small squirts of dish soap into a small dish. Add 2–3 drops of food coloring, and mix with the paintbrush.

- Repeat step 1 in new dishes to mix one or more additional colors.

- Lay the plastic bag down flat on a hard surface.

- Paint shapes, pictures, or designs on top. (Or slide a drawing or picture underneath to trace it.)

- Leave the clings to dry overnight.

- Peel up the clings, and stick them to a window. (If they dry out over time, dab a small amount of water on the softer side to help them cling again.)

105 HOW TO
SING YOURSELF TO SLEEP

Sing this lullaby to the tune of "The ABC Song." Then write your own song to sing yourself to sleep.

While in bed I close my eyes,
But I'm not bored—there's a surprise!
In my mind, I can see sheep,
And penguins, too, so I can't sleep.
Cakes with slime and plastic flies,
Robots, too—they've won a prize.
Rainbow parrots in disguise,
Volcanoes, snowballs, and French fries.
Amazing things I see each night,
As soon as I turn out the light.
Each night, I dream a new surprise,
That's why I love to close my eyes.

What do you want to dream about? Add your ideas to your own song!

106 HOW TO
KEEP A DREAM JOURNAL

As you sleep, your breathing, heart rate, and even *brain waves* slow down. Then, when you enter dream sleep, your brain waves speed back up. Most people have several dreams per night—but forget them. Record your dreams right when you wake up to keep them forever.

Notebook
Writing and drawing tools

- Before you go to sleep, place your notebook and writing tools by your bed.
- When you wake up, write and draw what you remember.

Many people dream they can fly, or have magical powers!

WHAT PEOPLE OR CHARACTERS WERE IN YOUR DREAM?

WHAT WAS THE SETTING?

WHAT HAPPENED?

WHAT ELSE DID YOU SEE OR HEAR?

HOW DID YOU FEEL?

HOLD TO FOLD A POCKET JOURNAL

Make a pocket journal for your day, your week, a trip, a big event, or a gift. It takes just one sheet of paper!

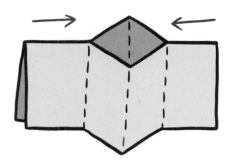

Sheet of paper

Scissors

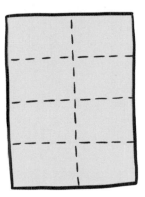

- Fold the top of the paper down to fold it in half.

- Fold the paper in half again so that it is in quarters.

- Fold the paper in half one last time. Press tightly so that the folds are flat.

- Unfold it so that you see eight equal boxes.

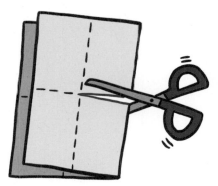

- Fold the top of the sheet of paper down again to fold it in half. Use scissors to make one small cut on the high-lighted line.

- Fold the paper in half the other way—the long way. Press the ends in so that the cut in the middle opens up.

- Push until the ends touch, and press the paper into a flat book shape.

STICK YOUR THUMB THROUGH YOUR EAR

TIP: Practice in the mirror until your prank is quick and easy.

You only need your hand and your ear for this gross-looking prank.

Choose the ear you want to use, and turn your head to the side so that your audience can't see it.

Take your hand on the same side, and open it wide. Place it behind your ear with your palm facing out.

Gently pinch the top of your ear between your thumb and your hand.

Still holding your ear, flip your hand down so that your palm is facing down.

Reach your pointer finger back, and pick up the lower lobe of your ear. Pinch it against your thumb.

Turn your head to show your thumb through your ear to your audience. (Wiggle your thumb, and make a shocked face to complete the trick!)

SHORT-SHEET A BED

Short-sheeting a bed is a simple prank: By pinning and tucking the sheets in a special way, you can surprise whoever hops in. The bed will seem too short!

> A bed with a fitted sheet, flat sheet, and a comforter or blanket

- Put the fitted sheet, with the elastic corners, on the bed normally.
- Lay the flat sheet on so that it is even all the way around. But put the wide edge that normally goes at the top at the bottom.
- Tuck in the sheet tightly across the top and around the top two corners.
- Pull the wide edge (that is down at the bottom) up the bed, and place it about where the pillows will go, near the top.
- Tuck in both sides. (It should look as though you've made a small envelope on top of the bed.)
- Last, place a comforter or blanket on top to hide your handiwork.

FAKE SPILLED MILK

> Piece of foil
> Bottle of white school glue

- Place the foil on a hard surface, like on top of a book or table. Smooth it out so that it's flat.
- Use the glue to draw the wavy shape of a spill on the foil. Fill it solid with glue. (The thicker it is, the easier it will be to peel off when it dries.)
- Leave it alone to dry—smaller "spills" may dry overnight, while larger "spills" make take a full day.
- Peel off your "spill," and place it somewhere as a prank.

111 HOW TO
BLOW A BUBBLE

> Piece of chewing gum

- Chew a piece of gum, and use your tongue to make it flat inside your mouth.

- Push it up against the back of your teeth, like a wall.

- Still using your tongue, push a little pocket into the flat wall of gum.

- Take a breath, and blow air into the pocket.

- It takes some practice to become an expert! Do the steps again, and puff up your cheeks when you blow.

112 HOW TO
BLOW A COLORFUL BUBBLE WORM

> Empty and clean recycled plastic water bottle (with the lid off)
>
> Clean sock (find one that is missing its match or that you've outgrown)
>
> Rubber band
>
> Bubble mix in a bowl
>
> Scissors
>
> Optional: food coloring

- With the help of an adult, cut off the bottom end of the water bottle.

- Pull the sock over the cut end of the bottle. Use the rubber band to secure it in place.

- Go outdoors or somewhere that is safe to get wet. (The bathtub works on a rainy or cold day.)

- Hold your bottle with the sock in your bowl of bubble mix until the sock is soaked.

- Put your lips on the open drinking spout of the bottle, and blow. (Make sure not to suck in or you might get some bubble mixture in your mouth—yuck!)

- Add 3–4 drops of any color of food coloring onto the end of your sock. Now dip and blow!

113 HOW TO
MAKE THE BEST BUBBLE KIT

½ cup of liquid dish soap

Bowl

Spoon

3 tablespoons of corn syrup

Pipe cleaner

Airtight container

Store your bubble mix in an airtight container for 1–2 weeks.

- Pour 1 ½ cups of water and the dish soap into your bowl. Mix slowly with a spoon—you want to avoid creating small bubbles and foam.

- Add the corn syrup, and stir slowly again.

- Bend your pipe cleaner in half. Starting at the middle, bend a small shape: like a circle, square, or heart.

- Twist the two extra ends together to form a handle.

- Go outdoors, dip the wand into the bubbles, and BLOW!

114 HOW TO
MAKE A GIANT BUBBLE WAND

2 twist ties

Masking tape

2 wooden dowels (about 1 foot long), chopsticks, or sticks

Piece of string or yarn (as tall as you are)

Washer or nut

Bowl of bubble mix

- Bend both twist ties in half. Use tape to secure each twist tie to the end of a dowel, forming a loop.

- Thread your string through both loops, add the washer, then tie it closed.

- Outdoors, hold the ends of your dowels and dip the string and washer into the bubble mix.

- Carefully lift the dowels and spread them apart, watching the bubble film stretch across the string. Take a step so that air can move against the film and form a bubble. Bring the dowels back together to close the bubble—and watch it float away!

MAKE THE EASIEST RUBBER BAND SLINGSHOT

> 1 or more small self-stick notes (or small pieces of paper)
>
> Scissors
>
> Rubber band

- Fold your sticky note in half. Then fold it in half again into a long rectangle.

- Unfold the sticky note— you should see four long rectangles. Cut them out.

- Take one long rectangle, and fold it in half. Fold it in half two more times until you have a small *V*-shaped fold. Fold the other rectangles the same way.

- Wrap the rubber band around your pointer and middle finger of one hand.

- With your other hand, pick up one folded sticky note. Place the *V* shape around the front of the rubber band by the outside of your hand.

- Pull it back, through your fingers and toward your palm. Then let it fly!

MAKE A RUBBER BAND BALL

> About 100 rubber bands of any shape and size

- Sort your rubber bands into two piles: large and small.

- Loop three large rubber bands around your thumb, and fold them up in half two or three times. Take them off your thumb, and use one small rubber band to hold them together tightly.

- Wrap one small rubber band at a time around the ball you've made. Roll the ball around in your hands as you add rubber bands to help it form a round shape. Each rubber band should be tight, so you may have to wrap it around multiple times. Also turn the ball so that each rubber band you add is going a different direction.

- As the ball gets bigger, wrap your larger rubber bands around it.

MAKE A FIZZY BATH BALL

Pop one of these into your next bath and you'll see why another name for these bath balls is bath *bombs*!

½ cup baking soda

2 teaspoons cornstarch

2 tablespoons citric acid

2 tablespoons Epsom salt

2 bowls: 1 large and 1 small, microwave-safe

Whisk

1 tablespoon of coconut oil

Airtight container

- With the help of an adult, pour the baking soda, cornstarch, citric acid, and Epsom salt into the large bowl. Mix with the whisk.

- Scoop your coconut oil into the small microwave-safe bowl, and melt it in the microwave. Start with about 20 seconds, and add 5 more seconds as needed until it is melted.

Citric acid is a powder that's naturally found in citrus fruits and often used as a preservative. When you combine this acid with baking soda (a base), you get a chemical reaction—carbon dioxide gas bubbles form.

Add a few drops of essential oil or water-soluble dye.

- Slowly pour the coconut oil into the large bowl of other ingredients. Add a few drops of water (and watch it fizz!).

- Mix well with your hands, taking care that the coconut oil isn't too hot. Play with it like sand—you want a small ball that sticks together. If the mixture is too dry, add a few more drops of melted coconut oil and keep mixing.

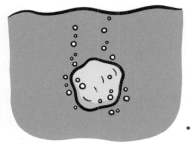

- Just like packing a snowball, scoop a small handful of the mixture into your palm and form a small ball, about the size of a rubber bouncy ball. You should be able to make 5–7.

- Dry the bath balls for 2 days.

- Pop one or two into a bathtub full of water! Store the rest in an airtight container to use later.

MAKE NO-BAKE COOKIES

Let's make chocolate peanut butter cookies.

2 tablespoons of butter

¼ cup of milk

2 tablespoons of cocoa powder

1 cup of sugar

Large microwave-safe bowl

Spoon

¼ cup peanut butter (or a nut-free alternative)

1½ cups of quick-cooking rolled oats

Plate

Wax paper

- Place the butter, milk, cocoa powder, and sugar into the bowl, and stir.

- With the help of an adult, microwave on high for 45 seconds. Be careful—the mixture may be hot.

- Stir the mixture, and microwave again for 15 seconds. Continue stirring and microwaving in short bursts until the mixture is melted.

- Stir in the peanut butter and oats.

- Line your plate with a piece of wax paper.

- Place large spoonfuls of the mixture onto the wax paper, and flatten them like cookies.

- Place the cookies in the refrigerator or freezer until cool. This should take about 20–30 minutes.

119 HOW TO
MAKE TWO-INGREDIENT COOKIES

Let's bake banana oatmeal cookies.

> 1 ripe banana
>
> Bowl
>
> ¾ cup of quick-cooking rolled oats
>
> Fork
>
> Baking tray
>
> Nonstick cooking spray
>
> Optional: pinch of salt

- With the help of an adult, preheat your oven to 350°F.
- Peel the banana, and place it in a bowl with the oats. (Optional: Add a pinch of salt.)
- Mash them together with a fork.
- Coat your baking tray with nonstick spray.
- Place a large forkful of the mixture onto a baking tray, and press to flatten it a bit. Do this until all the mixture is on the tray. (It should make 6–8 small cookies.)
- With the help of an adult, bake the cookies for 15–17 minutes.
- Let them cool—then share and enjoy.

> Break the two-ingredient rule, and add a small handful of chocolate chips, raisins, or coconut!

120 HOW TO
MAKE THREE-INGREDIENT COOKIES

> 1 cup creamy peanut butter (or a nut-free alternative)
>
> ½ cup brown sugar
>
> Egg
>
> Spoon
>
> Baking tray
>
> Bowl

- With the help of an adult, preheat your oven to 350°F.
- Place the peanut butter and brown sugar in a bowl. Crack in the egg.
- Mix well with a spoon.
- Place a large spoonful of the mixture on a baking tray, and press to flatten into a cookie shape. Repeat this until all the mixture is on the sheet. (It should make 10–12 cookies.)
- With the help of an adult, bake the cookies for 7–8 minutes.
- Let them cool—then share and enjoy.

121 HOW TO
JUMP A SNAKE

Jump over the snake the most times to win.

Jump rope

- Find a partner, and each holds one end of a jump rope on the ground.

- Wiggle it back and forth to make the snake move—but don't let go.

- Find another friend or two to jump over the snake. Can they make it without touching the snake?

- Take turns so that everyone gets a chance to jump. The player who jumps over the snake the most times without touching it wins.

122 HOW TO
LEAP ACROSS LAVA

3+

- Begin the game indoors or outdoors on a safe island: This can be anything up off the floor like a chair, bed, rock, or stump.

- Select your escape: You might choose to reach the door or find safe transport to a set of stairs, another chair, a patio, or a log.

- Journey from your island to your escape. Jump, hop, stretch, use pillows or towels—but remember the rules:

> RULE #1: THE GROUND IS LAVA!
>
> RULE #2: WHATEVER YOU DO, DON'T TOUCH THE LAVA!
>
> RULE #3: WELL, OF COURSE, THE GROUND ISN'T *REALLY* LAVA. IT'S JUST *PRETEND* LAVA. SO IF YOU *DO* TOUCH IT, RETURN TO YOUR SAFE ISLAND AND LEAP AGAIN.

HOW TO
MAKE A PAPER SNAKE

2 sheets of paper

Scissors

Tape

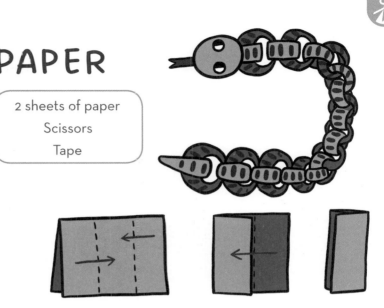

Fold the top of a sheet of paper down to fold it in half.

Then fold it into thirds: Fold in one side first, then the other side on top of it.

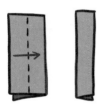

Fold the paper in half to form a long rectangle. Press hard to crease it. Then unfold the whole paper.

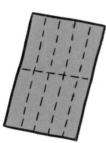

You should see 12 rectangle sections. Do this with the other sheet of paper, too, so you have 24 sections in all.

Cut off a long strip made of 2 sections. Draw and decorate a tail, and cut it out.

Cut off a long and wide strip made of 4 sections. Draw and decorate a head (with a tongue!), and cut it out.

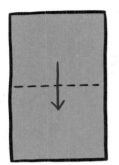

Decorate the rest of the 18 body sections, and cut them out.

To assemble your snake, make a loop of each section and tape it in place. Continue adding loops until all 18 are connected. Add your head at one end, taping it underneath. Add your tail at the other end.

HOW TO

FINGER KNIT WITH ONE FINGER

Finger knitting is a simple way to create a thick woven cord with no tools—start learning with just one finger.

Ball of yarn

Scissors

Make a loop around your thumb and pointer finger with the end of your yarn.

With your thumb and pointer finger, reach through the loop and grab the yarn that is still attached to the ball. Pull it tight. (You've just made a slipknot.)

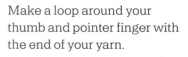

Place the loop on your pointer finger and adjust it so that it fits loosely. (If you are right-handed, place the loop around your left pointer finger, and vice versa.)

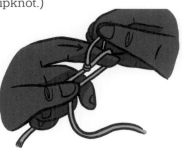

With your other hand, pick up the yarn that is still at-tached to the ball and wrap it around your finger one time.

Pick up the lower loop, and pull it over the higher loop, off your finger.

Start again, repeating step 3: Wrap the yarn around your finger, then pull off the lower loop.

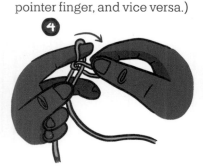

Keep going. When your cord is finished (long enough for a ring, bracelet, necklace, or other project), cut off the ball of yarn.

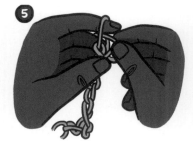

Take the loose piece of yarn, and thread it through the loop on your finger. Pull it tight until you have a secure knot.

FINGER KNIT WITH FOUR FINGERS

Ball of yarn
Scissors

Finger knit with all four fingers for a bigger challenge and a wider and more interesting cord.

With the help of an adult, tie a loose knot to attach a loop of yarn around your pointer finger. (If you are right-handed, tie the yarn around your left pointer finger, and vice versa.)

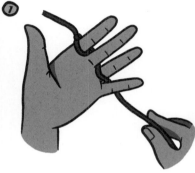

Pull the yarn behind your middle finger, over your ring finger, and behind your pinkie.

Then loop back: Pull the yarn around your pinkie, and weave back toward your pointer finger. You should have one loop around each finger.

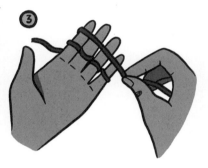

Pull the yarn across the front of all four fingers. One at a time, starting with your pinkie, pull the bottom loop on each finger over the top loop and off your fingers. Leave all the top loops in place. When you are done, you should have one loop around each finger.

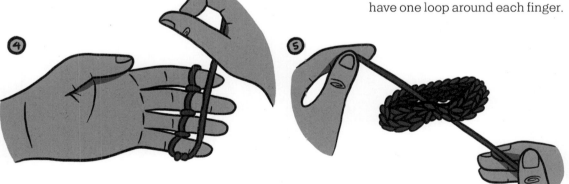

Now, pull the yarn across the front of all four fingers again, going in the other direction. One at a time, starting with your pointer finger, pull the bottom loop on each finger over the top loop and off your fingers. Again, you should be left with one loop around each finger.

Repeat until your cord is finished. Cut off the ball of yarn. Take the loose piece of yarn, thread it through the loop on each finger, and pull each loop off your hand. Then tie a knot.

MAKE SUGAR ORNAMENTS

1 cup of sugar

1 tablespoon of glitter

Bowl and spoon

Wax paper

Cookie cutters (any shape and size—you'll need about 8 small or 4 large)

4-8 paper clips (small ones work best)

Piece of string or ribbon for each cookie cutter (each about 8 inches long)

- Mix the sugar, glitter, and 4 teaspoons of water in a bowl until it looks like wet sand. (It may look too dry, but do not add more water.)

- Place one piece of wax paper on your work surface. Lay the cookie cutters on top.

- Use the spoon to scoop the sugar mixture into the cookie cutters. Use your fingers to pack the sugar down tightly. Each should be about ½ inch thick.

- Lift off the cookie cutters. Do not pick up or move the sugar mixture.

- Press a paper clip into the middle of the top of each shape until just a small loop is sticking out. Press down any sugar mixture that comes loose.

- Let it dry for a whole day—about 24 hours.

- When the shapes are dry, peel them off the wax paper and tie a piece of string through each paper clip loop. Hang them or give them as gifts.

**Your ornament is actually a sugar cube!
It must stay dry or it will lose its shape.**

CREATE YOUR OWN CRAYONS

> Small pile of used or broken crayons
>
> Silicone ice cube tray (or a muffin tin)
>
> Baking tray
>
> Nonstick cooking spray
>
> Toothpick

- With the help of an adult, preheat your oven to 250°F.

- Peel the labels off the crayons.

- Lightly coat the silicone tray with nonstick spray.

- Divide the crayons into the tray. Group by color or mix them up. (If any crayons are too large to fit, break them into pieces.)

- With the help of an adult, place the ice cube tray on a baking tray and into the oven for approximately 10–12 minutes. When the wax is melted, remove the baking tray.

- While still hot, use your toothpick to carefully swirl the colors. (Be careful with the hot wax.)

- Let the new crayons sit overnight to ensure that they are cool enough to use. (Or place them in the refrigerator or freezer to cool them down more quickly.)

MAKE YOUR OWN SOAP

> Glycerin soap blocks (usually sold in craft stores)
>
> Microwave-safe container with a pouring spout (like a glass measuring cup)
>
> Muffin tin
>
> Small plastic toys

What else could go in your soap? A coin, a pinecone, or glitter? Use your imagination!

- With the help of an adult, place a small handful of glycerin cubes in the microwave-safe container.

- Microwave them on high for 30 seconds. If you still see chunks, melt an additional 10 seconds. (This usually takes just over 1 minute.) Be careful—the melted glycerin will be very hot.

- Pour the glycerin into the cups of the muffin tin one at a time, filling each only about halfway.

- Put the muffin tin in the freezer for 10 minutes.

- Remove the muffin tin, and place a toy in each cup.

- Repeat the first 3 steps, this time filling each cup (on top of the toy) close to the top.

- Put the muffin tin back in the freezer until the soaps are cool and hard—30 minutes or more.

- Remove the muffin tin, and carefully turn it upside down. Tap the back to pop out the soaps.

129   HOW TO
CRAFT YOUR OWN HARMONICA

3 rubber bands

2 craft sticks (natural wood, not colored)

Scissors

Plastic straw

- Wrap the thickest rubber band around one craft stick the long way.

- Cut two pieces of straw, each just a little wider than the craft stick.

- Place one straw piece under the rubber band at one end of the craft stick.

- Place another craft stick on top.

- Wrap a second rubber band around both craft sticks, right next to the straw.

- Place a second straw piece at the other end of the craft sticks. (It will be on *top* of the long rubber band, but the top craft stick should hold it in place.)

- Wrap the last rubber band around both craft sticks at this end, right next to the straw.

- Blow, and listen to what happens.

130   HOW TO
MAKE A MUSICAL HORN

New garden hose (about 12 feet long)

Utility knife

Funnel

Duct tape

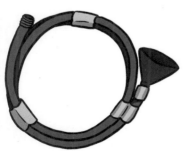

- Ask an adult to prepare the hose:

  - Sanitize one metal end. (This will be your mouth-piece.)

  - Cut off the other metal end with the utility knife.

- Push the funnel into the cut end until it is tightly in place. Use duct tape to secure it.

- Tear off three more large pieces of duct tape. Curve the hose into a few big loops. Secure it with the tape.

- Now you are ready to play: Press your lips tightly together, and blow into the metal end. You should feel your lips shake back and forth as you play.

Use a smaller or larger funnel to see how the sound changes.

MAKE AN ACCORDION BOOK

Sheet of paper
Quarter
Glue stick

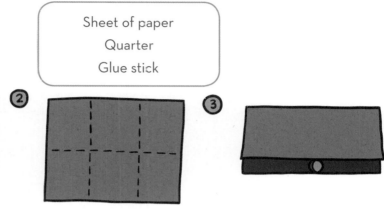

① First make a series of creases: Fold a sheet of paper in half the long way and then unfold it.

② Fold the paper into thirds the other way. Unfold it to make six equal pieces.

③ Place a quarter on the bottom of the paper. Fold the top down to meet the quarter, and crease it. Unfold it, put the quarter at the top. Fold the bottom up, and crease it.

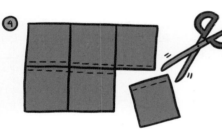

④ You should now have a paper with six large pieces and three lines in the middle.

⑤ Cut along the marked lines so that you have six equal pieces with tabs.

Cut the tab off one piece. This will be your cover.

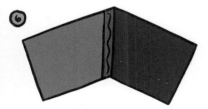

⑥ Glue the tab of another piece, and attach it to the cover, forming a V shape. Continue gluing tabs and adding pieces to your book.

⑦ Glue the pages so that the book goes back and forth, like an accordion. Use it like a journal or a notebook. For a longer book, fold another sheet of paper. And then another! Add as many pages as you like.

MAKE YOUR OWN LAVA LAMP

It looks like MAGIC, but it's actually SCIENCE!

Inside an antacid tablet is sodium bicarbonate (a base) and citric acid (an acid). When water is added, an acid-base reaction occurs and carbon dioxide gas is formed. This gas is less dense than the oil or water, so it floats to the top, taking some of the colored water with it!

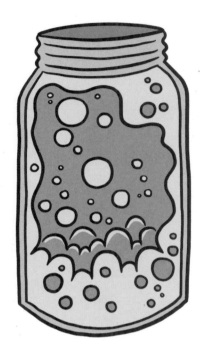

Vegetable oil

Clear bottle or jar (like a recycled plastic water bottle or a glass Mason jar)

Food coloring

Antacid tablet

Do not put a lid on your lava lamp until the reaction is completely finished.

- With the help of an adult, pour vegetable oil into the container until it is about ⅔ full.

- Pour water in until the liquid is about 1 inch from the top.

- Add 3–5 drops of food coloring.

- Break up an antacid tablet with your hands. Slowly add the pieces. (If your lava lamp slows down, add more antacid to fire it back up.)

133 HOW TO
ERUPT A VOLCANO

Gather your materials, and take them outdoors to an area that is safe to get covered in "lava."

Empty and clean recycled plastic water bottle (or other plastic or glass bottle similar in size)

Volcano materials: sand or dirt from outdoors, foil, or clay

Funnel

3 spoonfuls of baking soda

2 drops of dish soap

¾ cup of white vinegar

Optional for in your volcano: food coloring, glitter, sprinkles, confetti

Optional for around your volcano: small plastic toys

- Build a volcano around the bottle: sand, dirt, clay, or sculpted foil are good options. Get creative—add small plastic toys! Make sure you do not cover the top of the bottle.

- Take the lid off the bottle, and place the funnel inside.

- Pour in the baking soda first. Then pour in ¾ cup of water.

- Squirt in 2 drops of dish soap. (Optional: Add food coloring, glitter, sprinkles, or confetti now.)

- Quickly pour in the vinegar, and remove the funnel. Stand back!

TELL TIME WITH THE SUN

On a sunny day, use the shadow from a sundial to tell time.

> On cloudy days, or when the sun is directly overhead, you may not see a shadow. Look again a few hours later or when the weather changes.

> Thick stick, as short as 1 foot, but not taller than you
>
> 12 smooth stones
>
> Permanent marker

- Find a place in the dirt or grass to make a small hole with the stick. Bury the end tightly a few inches down so that it stands up straight.

- Find the stick's shadow and place a rock there, a foot or two away from the stick.

- Check the time on a watch or clock, and write the nearest hour on the rock, say, "7 o'clock."

- Continue to check in on your sundial throughout the day (and the next day), and add labeled rocks.

- When your sundial is complete, use it to tell time.

As the Earth spins, the sun appears to move across the sky. This makes the shadow move at a predictable speed around your sundial.

135 HOW TO
REMEMBER THE ORDER OF THE PLANETS

Memorize this poem and you'll *always* remember the order. Draw your own picture to prove it!

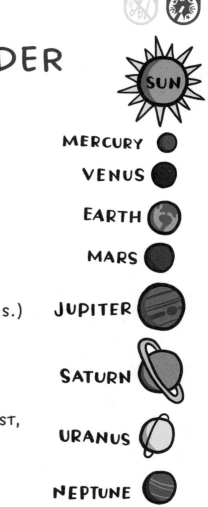

NOW EIGHT PLANETS ORBIT THE SUN,

MERCURY IS THE CLOSEST ONE.

THEN THERE'S VENUS, EARTH, AND MARS.

(EARTH, OF COURSE, IS THE ONE THAT'S OURS.)

THOSE INNER PLANETS ARE MADE OF ROCK.

THE OUTER PLANETS, NEXT, ARE NOT:

THERE'S JUPITER AND SATURN, AND ALMOST LAST,

URANUS AND NEPTUNE—ALL MADE OF GAS.

136 HOW TO
REMEMBER YOUR DIRECTIONS

The cardinal directions are the four main directions on a compass.

To remember each direction, make up a silly saying with the letters as they go around the compass clockwise:

137   HOW TO
WRITE A LETTER TO A PEN PAL

Pen pals are people who write letters back and forth. Sometimes a pen pal is a friend, and sometimes a pen pal is someone you don't know very well (or at all) who becomes your friend.

Paper

Envelope

Stamp

Writing tools (pencils, pens, markers, or crayons)

Ask someone to be your pen pal. You could pick:

- Someone at your school.

- A friend who moved away.

- A relative who lives in another place.

- Or ask an adult if they know of someone your age who may be interested.

Write the first letter. Share things about yourself: like your name, your family, and things you like to do and eat.

- Ask questions, too: like about where they live, their favorite books, or their school.

- Ask the receiver to write back if they'd like to be your pen pal.

Stamp it, mail it, and wait. Or send an email instead! (Hint: The postal service takes longer than email. That's why it's called *snail mail*!) Read your pen pal's letter and then write one back.

Keep writing back and forth. You've made a pen pal!

138   HOW TO
MAKE A FRIENDSHIP BRACELET DISK

With this disk, braid beautiful seven-strand friendship bracelets with ease!

Bowl, jar, or cup with about a round 4-inch diameter opening or lid

Thin cardboard (like from a cereal box)

Scissors

Pencil

Drawing tools (pens, markers, or crayons)

- Place the round shape onto the cardboard, and trace a circle.

- Use scissors to cut it out.

- Draw a small circle in the middle—a little larger than your finger. Cut it out with the help of an adult.

- Use your pencil to draw four marks on the circle: top, bottom, right, and left. Now draw four more marks, one in the middle of each of these.

- Use your scissors to make a small cut on each line.

BRAID A FRIENDSHIP BRACELET

Friendship bracelet disk

3 or more colors of satin rattail cord or embroidery floss (1–2 mm wide works great)

Scissors

Clear tape

- Cut seven pieces of cord: Hold your arms wide in front of you, and make each piece about that length.

- Stack the seven cords together so that they are even at the top. Tie a tight knot 1–2 inches down.

- Place the knot just through to the back of the hole in your friendship bracelet disk, and tape it in place.

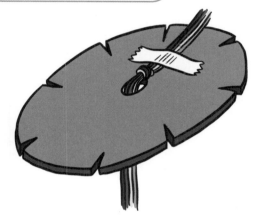

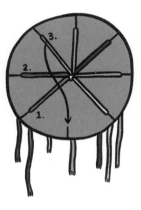

- Flip the disk over. Pull the seven strings out to the edges of the disk, and set them each in one slot (any slot).

- Turn the disk so that the one empty slot at the bottom faces you.

- With your left hand, count up to the left: 1, 2, 3. Pick up the third string, and pull it down to set it in the empty slot.

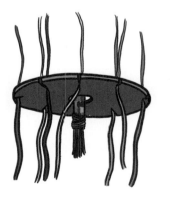

- Repeat the previous two steps.

- After a few minutes, you'll start to see the pattern of the braid forming through the hole and extending out the back. (Remove the tape at this point.) Use your fingers to untangle the long strings under the disk as you work.

- When your braid is as long as you want (for a key chain, bracelet, or other use), tie several knots to securely end the braid.

140 HOW TO
PLAY HOT AND COLD

> An object to hide indoors or outdoors (this can be almost anything: a stuffed animal, a shoe, a spoon, or a pinecone)

- Have the hider hide the object. (No peeking!)
- Now the seeker starts their search.
- The hider uses words to describe how close or far the seeker is from the object:

"YOU'RE COLD" MEANS YOU ARE FAR AWAY.

"YOU'RE GETTING WARMER" MEANS YOU ARE GETTING CLOSER.

"YOU'RE HOT" MEANS YOU ARE RIGHT BY IT.

- The hider continues giving hints until the seeker finds the object.
- Then switch roles and play again.

What other words can you use to describe close and far?

FROZEN SOLID / on Neptune / chilly / shivering / lukewarm / sweating / in the Sahara Desert / boiling / ON FIRE

141 HOW TO
MAKE A MELTING SCULPTURE

A freezing cold or snowy day is the perfect time to make art.

- Bundle up for a nature walk. Collect any small natural items you find.
- At home, fill the container with water until it's about an inch from the top.
- Arrange the natural items by dropping them into the water. Drop in the string so that about half of it is inside the water, too.
- Place the container in the freezer, or leave it outdoors if the temperatures are below freezing.
- The next day, or when it is frozen solid, gently remove the ice sculpture from the container.
- Use the string to hang it outdoors.

> Natural materials (like rocks, leaves, pinecones, acorns, flowers and petals, grasses, seeds, pieces of bark, feathers, shells, or small sticks)
>
> Plastic bowl or container
>
> Thick string or yarn (about 3 feet long)

142 HOW TO
TURN WATER INTO ICE INSTANTLY

> Sealed plastic bottle of water
> (Or a recycled bottle full of distilled water.
> Tap water likely will not work because there
> are too many impurities in it.)
>
> Handful of ice cubes
>
> Baking pan

- Place the bottle of water in your freezer for 3–4 hours. It should be extremely cold but not yet frozen.

- Pile some ice cubes onto a baking pan.

- Remove the water bottle from the freezer, open it and *slowly* pour the water directly onto the ice cubes.

143 HOW TO
MAKE YOUR OWN ICE POPS

> 4 small paper cups
>
> Ice pop liquids, like yogurt, fruit juice, lemonade, almond milk, or coconut water
>
> Foil
>
> 4 craft sticks (natural wood, not colored)
>
> Optional: sliced fruit like kiwis, bananas, or berries

- Fill each cup loosely halfway with sliced fruit. (Or skip this step if you'd just like to use liquids.)

- Fill each cup about ⅔ of the way with ice pop liquids. Mix flavors!

- Place one small piece of foil over the top of each cup, and fold it down and over the sides.

- Poke a craft stick down through the middle of the foil and into the liquid in each cup.

- Stand the cups upright in the freezer overnight.

- When the ice pops are frozen, remove the foil and tear away the paper cups.

PLAY FARKLE

Farkle is an easy-to-learn dice game. (It's also an excuse to yell "FARKLE" out loud.) .

> 6 dice
>
> Paper and pencil

- Decide on a player to go first. They roll all six dice.

- Use a score chart to add up the score. (Sometimes the score is 0.)

- Now the player must make **the big decision**:

  - Keep their score, and write it down.

  - Or, set aside one die, and roll the remaining five again for more points.

  - If the player rolls again and scores 0, they must yell, "Farkle!" Their total score for the round is 0. (They do not get to keep any points from their first roll.)

  - If the player rolls again and scores points, they must make **the big decision** again: Write down their combined points, or roll again with four dice to try for more points.

  - The player can keep going if they choose, with one less die each time, all the way down to one die.

- When a player's turn is over, the dice are passed to the left for the next player's turn.

- The first player to reach 10,000 points wins.

fives		50 points each
ones		100 points each
three of a kind		100 x the number on the dice example: 100 x 4 = 400 points
three ones in a roll		1,000 points
four of a kind		1,000 points
five of a kind		2,000 points
six of a kind		3,000 points
three pairs		1,500 points
a full run!		1,500 points

Any roll not included on the chart is worth 0 points. For example: 2, 2, 3, 3, 4, 5.

PLAY CENTENNIAL

Travel up and down the board by rolling the dice and counting your moves.
Be the first player to return back to 1 to win.

Paper and pencil

2 unique game board markers (like coins, small toys, or rocks)

3 dice

Draw and number your game board on a sheet of paper:

Both players' board markers start on the ★. The first player rolls all three dice together. They are looking for a 1 to move their piece to 1. They will need to go in order, so next they are looking for 2, then 3, 4, etc.

NUMBERS CAN BE USED ONLY ONE TIME PER ROLL.

NUMBERS ON TWO OR THREE DICE CAN BE ADDED TOGETHER.

FOR EXAMPLE, IF THEY ROLL 1, 1, 1: THEY CAN MOVE TO 1, AND THEN FOR THE REMAINING DICE, 1+1=2, SO THEY CAN MOVE TO 2.

IN LATER TURNS, THE ADDING HELPS TO GET TO HIGHER NUMBERS. FOR EXAMPLE: 1, 5, 6 = 12.

If they can move at all on their turn, they get to roll again. If they cannot move, it is the other player's turn.

The first player to travel from 1 up to 12 and then *back* to 1 wins.

146 HOW TO
GROW YOUR OWN OAK TREE

An acorn is a seed from an oak tree.

- Soak the acorns in a bowl of water for 24 hours. Throw away any that float.

- Fill the plastic bag with dirt, and add the acorns. Seal the bag.

- Place the bag in your refrigerator for 2 weeks. (Growing roots for new trees takes time!)

- Open the bag, and check the acorns for the start of taproots—small roots growing from the bottoms. Place any acorns without taproots back in your refrigerator, and check in another week.

- When you see small taproots, hold the acorn with the root facing down. Press three toothpicks in evenly around the middle.

- Fill the jar with water and balance the acorn across the top, with the taproots submerged. Place it near a window with natural light.

- Refill your jar with water as needed, and watch your new tree grow! Plant it after more roots and leaves appear.

> 5 or more acorns (pick ones without any holes or cracked shells)
>
> Bowl
>
> Resealable plastic bag
>
> Dirt or potting soil
>
> 3 toothpicks
>
> Glass jar (can be recycled)

147 HOW TO
WHISTLE WITH AN ACORN CAP

Grab a clean acorn when they fall this autumn.

- Pop the nut off the acorn. You will just need the cap, called a cupule.

- Make two fists, and hold them together with your thumbs touching.

- Place the cupule, with the inside facing you, right underneath the top of your thumbs.

- Bend your thumbs, creating a small Y shape with your knuckles still together.

- Wet your lips. Place them on your knuckles.

- Blow through the opening at the top of the Y. Each acorn cupule is different, so move your fingers slightly in, out, more bent, or less bent. It may take a few tries to get a good whistle.

> Acorn

TIP: Push the cupule down a little farther so that only a tiny bit can be seen at the top of the Y shape.

WHISTLE WITH A DANDELION

Pick a dandelion—skip the ones with yellow flowers. Instead, look for hollow stems that have a head full of white seeds, or just a seed head (the ball left when all the white seeds have blown away).

> Dandelion

- Break off the top and bottom of the dandelion stem, leaving a piece from the middle about as long as your hand.

- Use your thumb to flatten one end. Peel back the top just a little so that you have a slit on both sides.

- Place this split end in your mouth, and blow. Experiment with different positions for your lips until the split ends in your mouth vibrate, and whistling sounds are made.

WHISTLE WITH A BLADE OF GRASS

> Clean blade of grass
> (the wider the better)

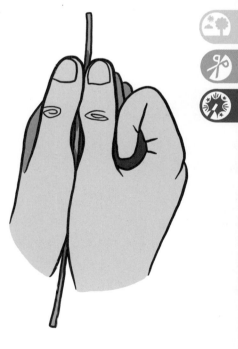

- Make two fists. Put them together with your thumbs facing you.

- Squeeze your thumbs together so that the tops and bottoms are touching.

- Place the blade of grass the long way between your thumbs.

- Blow into the space between your thumbs, just below your knuckles, where there is a gap and your thumbs can't touch. The grass here will vibrate.

- Form different positions for your lips until whistling sounds are made. It may take a few tries to get a sound you like.

150 HOW TO
MAKE YOUR OWN RAISINS

Did you know that raisins are dried grapes? Many raisins are made by drying grapes in the sun. But you can make raisins in your oven in any weather.

Bunch of grapes

Baking tray

Parchment paper

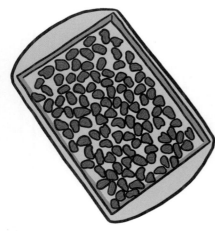

- Wash and dry one bunch of grapes. Pluck the grapes off the stem.

- Line the baking tray with parchment paper, and place the grapes on top.

- With the help of an adult, bake on the top rack of the oven at 200°F (or lower, if your oven is able). Check about every hour. Wait until most of the liquid has left the grapes—they should be smaller, shriveled up, and dried—but not crispy. Be careful not to let the bottoms burn.

- After approximately 2–4 hours (or when the raisins are done), remove them from the oven to cool.

- Eat or store in the refrigerator for up to 1 week.

Different colors of grapes make different colors of raisins!

151 HOW TO
MAKE NO-BAKE OATMEAL RAISIN BALLS

⅓ cup peanut butter (or a nut-free alternative)

3 tablespoons of honey

Microwave-safe bowl

1 cup of quick-cooking rolled oats

¼ cup of raisins (or dried cranberries or cherries)

Spoon

- With the help of an adult, place the peanut butter and honey into the bowl and microwave on high for 20 seconds. Be careful—the mixture may be hot.

- Add the oats and dried fruit into the bowl, and stir until well combined. Use your hands if the mixture gets too sticky.

- Use the spoon to scoop a large spoonful of the dough. Roll it around in your hands until it's in a tight ball and ready to eat.

- Store these in the refrigerator for up to 4 days.

SPEAK GIBBERISH

There are a few dialects, or versions, of gibberish. One of the most common uses the code "-idig."

Gibberish divides words into three groups:

ONE-SYLLABLE WORD THAT BEGINS WITH A CONSONANT:	ONE-SYLLABLE WORD THAT BEGINS WITH A VOWEL: AEIOU	MULTISYLLABLE WORD:
Example: pig or book	Example: ice or arm	Example: pencil or apple
Add -idig before the first vowel.	Add -idig before the first vowel.	Add -idig following the rules for *each* syllable.
example: pidigig or bidigook	example: idigice o⁻ idigarm	example: pidigencidigil or idigappidigle

Can you decode this? **Nidigow yidigou hidigave idiga nidigew lidigangidiguage!**

SPEAK OPPISH

Oppish is another dialect, or version, of gibberish. It uses the code "-op."

Oppish divides words into three groups:

ONE-SYLLABLE WORD THAT BEGINS WITH A CONSONANT:	ONE-SYLLABLE WORD THAT BEGINS WITH A VOWEL: AEIOU	MULTISYLLABLE WORD:
Example: pig or book	Example: ice or arm	Example: pencil or apple
Add -op before the first vowel.	Add -op before the first vowel.	Add -op before the first vowel *of each syllable.*
example: popig or bopook	example: opice or oparm	example: popencopil or opapopple

Can you decode this? **Opoppopish opis fopun topo sopay.**

HOW TO

MAKE A PAPER FORTUNE-TELLER

Square piece of paper
(see page 8)

Writing tools (pencils,
pens, markers, or crayons)

Optional: stickers

Fold the paper in half to form a triangle. Unfold it, and fold it in half the other way. Unfold it to see an *X*-shaped crease in the middle of the paper.

Fold one corner of the paper in to meet the middle. Then fold the other three corners in.

Flip the paper over.
Fold one corner of the square in to meet the middle. Then fold the other three corners in.

 FLIP  **FLIP**

Lay your fortune-teller on a table with the side with only an X facing up. Use colored stickers or pencils to label each flap with one color.

Flip your fortune-teller over to the side with an X and four slits. Use stickers or pencils to label each half of a flap with one number.

Open up each flap. Use stickers or a pencil to add a picture or message to each of the outer eight triangles. These will be the final fortunes when someone plays your game.

Fold it back together. On the *X*-only side, peel open the four flaps—insert your thumbs and fingers under them and push them up, like little spikes.

Instead of colors and numbers, label your fortune-teller with animals, foods, or sports. You can label and sticker your fortune-teller however you like!

PLAY WITH A PAPER FORTUNE-TELLER

Paper fortune-teller

- Insert your two thumbs and pointer fingers into the bottom of the spikes of your fortune-teller. Ask a friend to choose a color on one flap.

- When they choose a color, you will spell it out loud, moving the fortune-teller one time for each letter.

FIRST MOVE: WHILE KEEPING YOUR THUMBS TOGETHER AND POINTER FINGERS TOGETHER, MOVE YOUR FINGERS AWAY FROM YOUR THUMBS. THEN BRING THEM BACK.

SECOND MOVE: WHILE KEEPING YOUR RIGHT THUMB AND FINGER TOGETHER AND LEFT THUMB AND FINGER TOGETHER, MOVE YOUR RIGHT HAND AWAY FROM YOUR LEFT. THEN BRING IT BACK.

- Continue back and forth. If they selected red, you'd say "R-E-D" while moving the fortune-teller three times. After your last move, leave the fortune-teller open.

- Ask your friend to choose one of the four numbers visible inside.

- When they choose a number, you will count it out loud, moving the fortune-teller one time for each number. After your last move, leave the fortune-teller open.

- Ask your friend to choose one of the four numbers visible again.

- Take the fortune-teller off your thumbs and fingers and peel open the flap to reveal the fortune under their number.

PLAY PIG

Be quick to get your finger on your nose and avoid spelling *pig*!

> Deck of cards
>
> Paper and pencil

- Each player selects four cards of the same rank from the deck. (So four aces or four 2s, etc.)

- Choose one player to be the dealer. The dealer shuffles just the selected cards and gives each player four cards, facedown.

THE GOAL OF THE GAME IS TO COLLECT ONE FULL SET OF FOUR MATCHING-RANK CARDS, AND TO QUICKLY NOTICE WHEN SOMEONE ELSE DOES!

(If someone is dealt four of the same cards at the start—they win. Shuffle and play again.)

- To play, each player looks at their cards and selects one they don't want. When everyone is ready, say together, "Ready, set, pig!" At the word *pig*, each player passes their unwanted card to the left, facedown.

- Each player picks up their new card and reviews it. Then all the players repeat these steps to pass another card.

- This continues until someone has one full set of four matching-rank cards. That player quietly stops passing cards and places a finger on their nose.

- Any player who notices this should *also* stop passing and place *their* finger on *their own* nose. The last player to do so loses the round.

- The losing player writes a P as their score, and plays again. Each person who spells out the whole word *P–I–G* is eliminated.

157 HOW TO
PLAY CAT AND MOUSE

If you're the cat, you must catch all the mice. If you're a mouse, you must help the other mice make it to the mousehole.

- Choose one player to be the cat. The rest of the players are mice.

- Choose a location or object to be the mousehole—this could be a chair or a tree, for example.

- To start, the cat must cover their eyes and count to 10. The mice run (quietly!) and hide.

- Now the cat is on the hunt—they must catch every mouse they see with a gentle tag.

IF THE CAT CATCHES A MOUSE, THE MOUSE IS FROZEN. THEY CAN ONLY MOVE AGAIN IF ANOTHER MOUSE TAGS THEM.

IF THE MOUSE MAKES IT TO THE MOUSEHOLE, THEY ARE SAFE.

- If the cat catches all the mice—the cat wins! Or if all the mice make it to the mousehole—the mice win! Choose a new cat, and play again.

158 HOW TO
PLAY WHAT'S THE TIME, MR. WOLF?

If you are the wolf, sneaky timing can catch a player. If you are a player, sneaky moves can outfox the wolf!

- All players stand on a starting line outdoors. Select one player to be the wolf—they walk 10–12 paces away and face where they cannot see the others.

- The rest of the players ask together, "What's the time, Mr. Wolf?"

- The wolf flips around and peeks at the players while announcing: "6 o'clock!" The wolf can announce any time they want, and then they turn back around.

- The players run toward the wolf to match the time: 6 o'clock equals six steps. They count aloud as they run: 1, 2, 3, 4, 5, 6. Then together they ask again, "What's the time, Mr. Wolf?"

- The wolf can announce another time if they want the players to come closer. Or, if the wolf guesses they are close enough, they can flip around and announce, "Dinnertime!"

- The wolf runs and tries to tag any of the players before they safely reach the starting line. The first player the wolf catches is the new wolf.

159   HOW TO
PLAY TWO FACTS AND A FIB

The goal of this classic game, also called two truths and a lie, is to craft a believable fib. If the other players believe it—you win points.

- The first player shares three statements about themselves. These can be *anything*: favorite foods or pets, skills you have, places you've been, or more. Two must be true, and one must be made up.

I CAN STAND ON MY HEAD FOR 1 MINUTE.

I KNOW HOW TO MAKE PUDDING BY MYSELF.

MY FAVORITE ANIMALS ARE PEACOCKS.

- The other player (or players) are allowed one guess which statement was made up. If they believe your fib—you win a point.

- Continue taking turns—the player with the most points wins.

160   HOW TO
CATCH KNUCKLEBONES

Knucklebones is a game that has been played for thousands of years. (It was traditionally played with small bones from the ankle of a sheep!) To play, you'll need to learn to throw and catch the small objects, which are called the bones.

> 5 small objects—dried beans, small stones, very small plastic toys, or other small objects (they cannot be round, like a ball)

- Begin with all five bones in the palm of your hand.
- Toss them up in the air.
- Quickly flip your hand over, and catch as many as you can on the *back* of your hand.
- Now toss the ones you caught up in the air again from the back of your hand.
- Quickly flip your hand over, and catch them in your palm.

Catching the bones takes *lots* of practice.

PLAY KNUCKLEBONES

There are many ways to play knucklebones. Once you've learned how to catch the bones, you are ready to play.

> 5 small objects—dried beans, small stones, very small plastic toys, or other small objects (they cannot be round, like a ball)

- Select one bone to be your taw. Toss the other four bones on the ground.
- Toss the taw in the air, and quickly pick up one bone. Grab the taw before it hits the ground. Then dump the bone you picked up to the side.

IF YOU DON'T MAKE IT, IT IS THE OTHER PLAYER'S TURN.

IF YOU MAKE IT, GO AGAIN, PICKING UP THE REMAINING BONES ONE AT A TIME.

- When you are done, play for twos: Toss the taw in the air. Quickly pick up two bones. Grab the taw before it hits the ground.
- Then do threes.
- When you get to fours, you will pick up all four bones at one time. The first player to do this wins the game.

Play these variations, too:

THROUGH THE ARCH

1. Form an arch with one hand: Hold your fingers together, and have them and your thumb all touch the ground, making an upside-down *U* shape.

2. Place four bones on the ground with your other hand. Then toss up the taw. Quickly knock or flick one bone through the arch. Grab the taw before it hits the ground. If you did it, your turn continues. If you missed, your turn is over.

3. Take turns. Whoever knocks all four bones through the arch first wins.

IN THE HOLE

1. Form a circle with the thumb and pointer finger of one hand, like a basket. Hold it a few inches off the ground.

2. Place four bones on the ground with your other hand. Then toss up the taw. Quickly grab one bone, and drop it in the hole. Grab the taw before it hits the ground. If you did it, your turn continues. If you missed, your turn is over.

3. Take turns. Whoever drops all four bones through the hole first wins.

162 HOW TO
PLAY RED LIGHT, GREEN LIGHT

Race through multicolor lights, and tag the traffic cop to win.

- Choose one player to be the traffic cop. Have the other players stand on a starting line 10 or more feet away.

- The traffic cop calls out different colors of lights:

GREEN LIGHT means run.	YELLOW LIGHT means walk.	RED LIGHT means stop. Any player who does not immediately stop for a red light is sent back to the starting line.

- The traffic cop can add twists to the game by making up new colors of lights:

ORANGE LIGHT could mean running with both feet and both hands on the ground.	BLUE LIGHT could mean hopping on one foot.	PURPLE LIGHT could mean running backward.

- The game is over when a player tags the traffic cop. Play again with the winner being the new traffic cop.

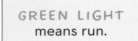

163 HOW TO
PLAY YES/NO BLACK/WHITE

Answer questions quickly without saying the forbidden words, all while asking questions that will trick the other player into saying them.

- One player begins the game as the interviewer. They can ask the other player any five questions they'd like. The goal is to trick the other player into saying *yes, no, black,* or *white.*

WHAT COLOR IS A ZEBRA?
ARE APPLES RED?
DO YOU LIKE HOT DOGS?

- The other player must answer the questions truthfully, but without saying the forbidden words. Each correct answer they give earns them 1 point:

A ZEBRA HAS DARK AND LIGHT STRIPES. (1 POINT!)	SOME APPLES ARE RED, AND SOME ARE NOT. (1 POINT!)	YES! I LOVE HOT DOGS. (0 POINTS, BUT 1 POINT FOR THE INTERVIEWER!)

- When one player says a forbidden word, the other player wins a point and the roles are switched. Continue taking turns as the interviewer. The player with the most points wins!

PLAY DOTS AND BOXES

Complete the most boxes to win.

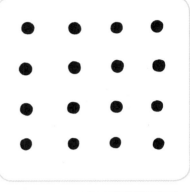

Sheet of paper

Writing tool for each player
(different colors work best)

Coin

On your paper, draw a
grid 4 dots across by
4 dots down. (There
should be 13 dots in all.)

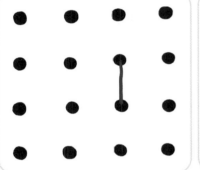

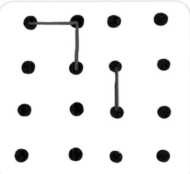

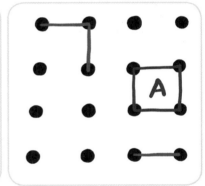

Flip a coin to see who goes
first. The first player uses their
pencil to draw a vertical or
horizontal line connecting any
two neighboring dots.

Then the second player does
the same, drawing a line anywhere on the board. Continue
taking turns and drawing
lines.

When a box on the board has
three lines as sides, the player
whose turn it is can draw the
fourth line to complete the
box. They write their initial
inside the box to mark it as
theirs *and* take an extra turn,
drawing the next line.

The game is done when all the available lines on the
board have been drawn. Players count up the boxes
with their initials. Whoever has the most wins.

Play again on a grid with *more* dots!

165 HOW TO
HOST A PENNY TOWER RACE

Large pile of pennies
(at least 25 for each player)

Timer

- Begin the game at a table, and place the pile of pennies in the middle.

- Start the timer. Each player must stack as many pennies as they can in 1 minute. The player with the highest stack when the timer goes off wins. How high can you stack pennies before they fall over?

Race again using different types of coins.

166 HOW TO
PLAY A PRANK WITH A PENNY

Penny

Bottle of glue

- Find a place to glue the penny to the ground. Pick a place that's safe (not near cars or moving bikes) and where the glue will not harm floors. It's best to do this prank outdoors, somewhere where people will see it—like a sidewalk, garage, or deck.

April 1 is April Fools' Day!

- Glue the penny to the ground. Step on it for a few seconds to help it stick tightly. Then let it dry.

- Watch and wait—who will fall for your prank?

167 HOW TO
TURN A PENNY GREEN

¼ cup of white vinegar

1 teaspoon of salt

Small bowl (made of anything but metal) and spoon

Handful of dull pennies

Old towel or paper towel

- Pour the vinegar and salt into the bowl, and stir to dissolve. It should be mixed in so that you no longer see it.

- Place a few pennies in the liquid, and watch what happens.

- After about 2 minutes, pull them out but *do not* rinse them.

- Place them on the towel to dry. Check back in 10 minutes, a few hours, and the next day.

MAKE A PENNY LOOK NEW

Pennies are made with two types of metals: zinc with a thin outer coating of copper.

¼ cup of white vinegar

1 teaspoon of salt

Small bowl (made of anything but metal) and spoon

Handful of dull pennies

- Pour the vinegar and salt into the bowl, and stir to dissolve. It should be mixed in so that you no longer see it.

- Place a few pennies in the liquid, and watch what happens.

- After about 2 minutes, pull them out and rinse them in the sink.

- Place them on the towel to dry.

It looks like MAGIC, but it's actually SCIENCE!

Over time, pennies stop looking like shiny copper—they get dull because they are covered in copper oxide. This happens when oxygen atoms (from the air) combine with the copper atoms on the surface of the pennies. The vinegar solution dissolved the copper oxide, revealing the shiny copper of the pennies. As the pennies sit exposed to the air, the copper atoms interact with both the oxygen and the leftover chlorine from the salt to form a blue-green compound called malachite.

2

169 HOW TO
PLAY PICKUP PENCILS

Pick up the most pencils to write your name as the winner.

| 12 or more pencils (sharpened or unsharpened) |

- Hold all the pencils in your hand so that they are vertical. Drop them all at once into a messy pile on a table or the ground.

- Choose a player to go first: Their goal is to pick up one pencil *without moving any other pencils* at all. If they succeed, they can go again (and again). If any other pencils move, even a little, their turn is over.

- Each player takes a turn until all the pencils are picked up. Whoever has the most pencils wins.

170 HOW TO
TALK LIKE A COWGIRL OR COWBOY

No time to make up a secret language? Talk to your friends like cowboys and cowgirls and y'all will be above snakes!

ROLL PAPER BEADS

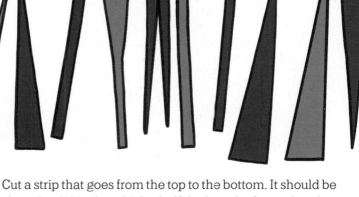

Magazine

Scissors

Toothpick

Glue stick

Optional: string or cord to make a necklace, bracelet, or key chain

- Choose a page of colors or textures you like in the magazine, and rip out the page.

- Cut a strip that goes from the top to the bottom. It should be about 1 to 1½ inches thick—half the length of your thumb or the whole length. Thinner strips make smaller beads, and wider strips make larger beads. It can be made of any straight or curved lines. Here are some ideas:

- Hold one end of the strip—the wide end if you have one. Wrap it tightly around the middle of a toothpick.

- Set it down, and use the glue stick along the inside of the rest of the strip.

- Tightly roll the glued paper around the toothpick.

- Pull the completed bead off the toothpick, and allow it to dry.

Repeat the steps to make more beads of different colors, shapes, and sizes. String them together to make a necklace, bracelet, or key chain.

172 **HOW TO**
PLAY CUCKOO

Be the last player holding a token to win *all* the tokens.

> Deck of cards
>
> 3 tokens for each player
> (these could be pennies, paper clips,
> or small wrapped candies)

- Choose a player to be the dealer. The dealer shuffles the cards and gives each player one card, facedown. Each player also needs three tokens.

- Each player looks at their card. The goal of the game is to *not* be left with the lowest card. From lowest to highest, the cards are:

Ace, 2, 3, 4, 5, 6, 7, 8, 9, 10, Jack, Queen, King

- The player on the left side of the dealer goes first. They can say **"Keep"** to keep their card or **"Cuckoo!"** to swap it. If they say **"Cuckoo!"** the player on *their left* must exchange cards with them.

    - (Except, if this player has the highest card, a king, they are allowed to say **"King!"** and keep their card. Then both players are stuck with what they have.)

- If they swap, the player with the new card can look at what they received. They can then decide to keep it or swap it with the person on *their* left.

- The game continues left around the circle until it gets back to the dealer. The dealer can either keep or swap. Since there is no one left to swap with, the dealer can discard and draw a new card from the deck.

    - (Except, if the dealer draws a king, they must say **"King!"** and lose a token.)

- Now it's time for the reveal: Everyone flips their cards over. The player with the lowest card loses a token. (If there is a tie, *both* players lose a token.)

- The player to the left of the dealer becomes the new dealer for the next round.

- When a player runs out of tokens, they are out of the game. The last player left with a token or more wins *all* the tokens.

MAKE PEANUT BUTTER AND JELLY SUSHI

Cutting board and butter knife

2 slices of bread

Rolling pin (or a can)

Spoon

Peanut butter
(or a nut-free alternative)

Jelly

- On the cutting board, cut the crusts off both slices of bread.
- Roll both slices flat with the rolling pin.
- Add a spoonful of peanut butter to one slice and a spoonful of jelly to the other. Spread them out with the knife.
- Place the slices together with the peanut butter and jelly on the inside.
- Roll up the slices into a tube.
- Cut the tube into four pieces. Stand the rolls up, like sushi, and enjoy!

Use chopsticks to eat your sushi!

MAKE JELL-O AND MARSHMALLOW SUSHI

8-by-8-inch baking pan

Nonstick cooking spray

3-ounce box of Jell-O

Microwave-safe bowl

Spoon

1 cup of small marshmallows

Cutting board and knife

- Coat the baking pan with nonstick spray.
- Dump the Jell-O and ½ cup of water into a microwave-safe bowl, and microwave on high for 90 seconds.
- With the help of an adult, remove the bowl and stir to dissolve the Jell-O. (If it doesn't dissolve, microwave on high for 20 seconds, then stir again.)
- Add the marshmallows to the bowl, and stir.
- Microwave for 1 minute, then stir again until they are fully melted.
- Pour the mixture into the pan, and cool in the refrigerator for 1 hour or more.
- Use the end of the spoon to "cut" around the edges of the pan to release your mixture.
- While still in the pan, tightly roll up the mixture into a tube.
- Place the tube on a cutting board, and slice into eight pieces. Stand the pieces up like sushi, and enjoy!

175 HOW TO
MAKE A SNOW ANGEL

- Lie down flat in the snow, and move your arms and legs up and down, back and forth.
- Customize your snow angel, too:

Add a halo!   **Add cowboy boots!**   **Add other accessories!**

176 HOW TO
PAINT SNOW

> Spray bottle
> Food coloring

- Take the lid off the spray bottle, and fill it ¾ of the way with water.

- Add ½ a bottle of food coloring. (Or adjust for the size of your spray bottle: The ratio is about 1 cup of water to ½ a bottle of food coloring.)

- Put the lid back on and shake.

- Head to the snow, and spray away! (Note: If your color isn't bright enough, add a bit more food coloring. Food coloring can stain clothes and other items, so spray this *at the snow* but not at people or other items.)

MAKE A 3D PAPER SNOWFLAKE

6 pieces of square paper
(see page 8—squares can
be any size as long as they
are all the same)

Scissors

Tape or glue stick

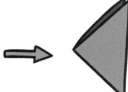

① Fold one paper square in half diagonally to make a triangle. Fold it in half again.

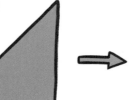

②  Use your scissors to cut three slits on either short side. Stop before you get to the other short side.

③ Unfold the paper. Fold in the two smallest triangles around your pinkie, and secure them with tape or glue. (Use a partner to help with this step if needed.)

FLIP ↻

④ Flip the whole paper over. Fold in the next two smallest triangles around your pinkie, and secure them with tape or glue.

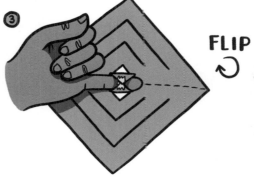

⑤ 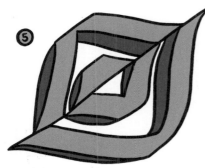 Do this two more times until all the triangles are secured. Repeat the steps with the five remaining square pieces of paper so that they are all cut and wrapped the same.

⑥ Arrange the six pieces in a circle to form your snowflake. One at a time, tape or glue each branch to the one next to it in two places: at the point in the middle and at the widest part.

MAKE A CARDBOARD CASTLE

Cardboard boxes and tubes of various sizes

Scissors

Drawing tools (colored pencils/pens, markers, or crayons)

String

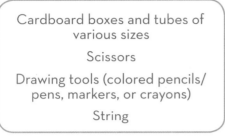

- Look at your cardboard, and decide if you can make a large castle (for you to fit inside) or a small castle (for your toys to fit inside).

- Select a main box to be the curtain wall. Fold in the bottom flaps to make a floor. Draw battlements around the top, and cut them out with scissors.

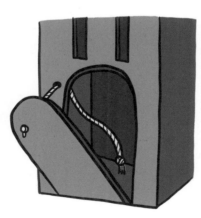

If you have any round cardboard, like paper towel or oatmeal tubes, add towers and flags.

- Draw arrow slits. With the help of an adult, cut them out.

- Draw a door. Cut out the top and sides so the bottom is still attached.

- Poke two holes with the scissors: one in the top of the door and one in the wall right next to the top of the door.

- Cut a piece of string that is twice the height of the door. Thread it through the holes, and tie knots on the front of the door and inside the castle. Pull the string to raise and lower your drawbridge.

MAKE A MINI CROWN

Toilet paper tube

Scissors

Markers

Hole punch

String

- Cut out about five triangles along the top of the tube to create a zigzag edge.

- Decorate the tube with markers.

- Punch two holes, one on each side of the bottom of the tube.

- Cut two pieces of string, each the distance from your elbow to your thumb.

- Tie one end of each string into one of the holes.

- Place the crown on the new king or queen's head. Tie the two hanging strings under their chin so that the crown stays in place.

BUILD AN INDOOR SANDCASTLE

Double or triple the batch to make a larger sandcastle.

4 cups of flour

½ cup of vegetable oil

Large plastic tub

Sand toys (or common objects like small plastic cups, measuring spoons, and a fork)

Airtight container

- Pour the flour and vegetable oil into your tub.

- Mix them with your hands for a few minutes until they are fully combined.

- Pack the mixture into the cups, and tap it out to make shapes. Use the measuring spoons to make small details, like windows or doors. Use the fork like a sand rake.

- Store your indoor sand in an airtight container for up to 1 week.

FLOAT A FROZEN BOAT

> Foil
>
> Small to medium-size plastic container (any shape)
>
> Wooden dowel (about 1 foot long) or chopstick
>
> Food coloring
>
> Sheet of paper
>
> Scissors
>
> Drawing tools (colored pencils/pens, markers, or crayons)
>
> Glue stick

- Tear off a sheet of foil that is large enough to cover the top of the container twice. Fold the foil in half. Use the wooden dowel to poke a hole through the middle.

- Fill the container ⅔ of the way with water. Add a few drops of food coloring, but do not mix it in. This will be your boat.

- Place the foil over the top, and insert the wooden dowel through the hole so that it is standing straight up. This will be your mast. Place the container in the freezer overnight or until it is frozen solid.

- Make your sail: Fold the sheet of paper in half. Using the fold as one side, draw two lines to form a triangle.

- Cut it out, and decorate it on both sides.

- When the boat is frozen, pop it out of the container. Add glue to the *inside* of the folded triangle, and attach the sail to your mast.

- Place your boat in a bowl of water, filled sink, bathtub, or puddle.

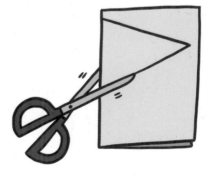

MAKE A PAPER BOAT THAT REALLY FLOATS

Wooden dowel (about 1 foot long) or chopstick

Pencil, pen, or permanent marker

Half-gallon paper carton (like from milk or juice)

Scissors

Sheet of construction paper

Glue (bottle or stick)

Small ball of clay

Optional: acrylic paint and paintbrush

- Use the wooden dowel as a straight edge to draw a line lengthwise down the middle of two opposite sides of the carton. This will divide it into two equal halves.

- Ask an adult to cut along the line and around the carton. You'll use one half and throw the other half away.

OPTIONAL: PAINT YOUR BOAT NOW, AND LET IT DRY OVERNIGHT.

- Draw a large triangle on the paper, and cut it out.
- Fold over one edge of the paper flag so that it wraps just over the wooden dowel. Leave the bottom of the wooden dowel hanging out the bottom, like a flagpole or mast.
- Place glue in the fold to keep the wooden dowel in place.
- Press your small ball of clay into the middle of the boat, and push the wooden dowel into it.
- Go float your boat.

183 HOW TO
PLAY AIR SOCCER

Earn the most points by getting your team's balloon over the scoring line to win.

Balloon

- This game is played outdoors with two teams of any number of players.

- Together the teams need to pick a playing space (anything large enough to run around in) and two scoring lines—one for each team to defend at either end of the playing space.

- The goal of the game is to hit the balloon over the other team's scoring line to earn a point.

- Kick, push, tap, or even blow the balloon. But you cannot grab it or hold it. You also cannot touch other players.

- Whichever team scores the most points wins.

Play with two balloons. Or three. Or more!

184 HOW TO
INFLATE A BALLOON WITH CANDY

Balloon

Funnel

Popping candy

Bottle of soda (12–20 ounces)

- Set up a place to work outdoors—this will be messy!

- Pick up the uninflated balloon, and put the funnel inside.

- Pour in 2–3 spoonfuls of candy.

- Open the soda. With the help of another person, stretch the opening of the balloon over the open soda top.

- Lift the balloon slowly up and wiggle it so that all the candy inside falls down into the soda. Watch the reaction!

185 HOW TO
MAKE A BALLOON SING

> Uninflated balloon

- Blow the balloon full of air, but do not tie it shut.
- Hold it in front of you—with both hands pinching the neck.
- Slowly pull your hands apart while stretching the neck of the balloon. Hold your fingers looser to let some of the air out of the balloon. Listen to the sounds as the air escapes through the tiny space you've made in the neck.
- Move your hands around to make different sounds—pull and squeeze the neck in different ways to make the balloon sing.

186 HOW TO
PLAY WATER BALLOON TOWEL TOSS

4+

In this outdoor game, catch the most water balloons to win. Dress to get wet!

> Towel for each team of two players
>
> Lots of water balloons

- Divide into teams of two players each. Each team holds one towel: The first player holds one short end, the second player holds the other short end. Stand about 6 feet between the teams.
- Place a water balloon in the middle of one towel.
- That balloon team slowly starts to swing their towel back and forth and count: "1, 2 . . ." On "3," both players lift their ends of the towel with a snap and send the balloon flying toward the other team.
- The other team moves their legs, arms, and towel to catch the balloon.

IF THEY CATCH IT, THEY EARN A POINT. THEY TAKE ONE STEP BACK TO INCREASE THE CHALLENGE.

IF THEY MISS IT, THE THROWING TEAM EARNS A POINT.

Repeat the steps to toss the balloon back.

MAKE PUMPKIN MUFFINS

Pumpkins you can eat!

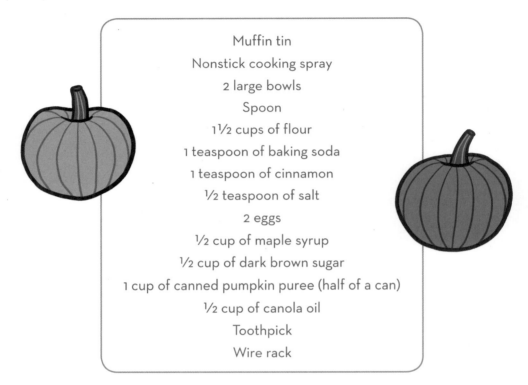

Muffin tin

Nonstick cooking spray

2 large bowls

Spoon

1½ cups of flour

1 teaspoon of baking soda

1 teaspoon of cinnamon

½ teaspoon of salt

2 eggs

½ cup of maple syrup

½ cup of dark brown sugar

1 cup of canned pumpkin puree (half of a can)

½ cup of canola oil

Toothpick

Wire rack

- With the help of an adult, preheat the oven to 350°F.
- Coat the muffin tin with nonstick spray.
- In the first bowl, mix the flour, baking soda, cinnamon, and salt.
- In the second bowl, mix the eggs, maple syrup, brown sugar, pumpkin puree, and canola oil.
- Pour the pumpkin mixture into the flour mixture, and stir until there are few lumps. Pour the mixture evenly between the 12 muffin cups.
- Bake for 18–22 minutes, or until a toothpick stuck into the top of a muffin comes out clean.
- Cool on a wire rack. Share and enjoy.

ROAST PUMPKIN SEEDS

1 small to medium-size pumpkin

Cutting board and knife

Bowl and spoon

Towel

Baking tray

2 tablespoons of olive oil

Pinch of salt

Spatula

Optional: Cinnamon, chili powder

Bigger pumpkins usually have bigger seeds. Often, smaller seeds taste better, so search for a smaller pumpkin.

- With the help of an adult, cut open the pumpkin.

- Using a spoon (or your hands!), scrape out the insides to remove the guts. (It's easy to get the seeds while you are carving a pumpkin, so you may make this around Halloween.)

- Place the guts in a bowl. Use your fingers to separate the stringy insides and throw them away. Only the seeds should be left in the bowl.

- Fill the bowl halfway with water, and wash the seeds, using your hands to remove any remaining pieces of the guts.

- Scoop the seeds out of the water, and dry them on a towel for about 1 hour.

- Place the dried pumpkin seeds on a baking tray. Toss them with the olive oil and salt. (You can also add a teaspoon of cinnamon or chili powder!)

- With the help of an adult, bake the seeds at 350°F. After 10 minutes, use a spatula to flip and stir them. Continue baking until they are crispy and golden brown. This depends on the size of the seeds, but it usually takes about 20 minutes total.

- Remove the sheet from the oven, and let the seeds cool. Then have a crunchy snack.

HANG A PLAY TENT FROM ONE TREE

Small ball (tennis ball, pet's toy ball, or Ping-Pong ball)

Flat bedsheet (the larger the better)

Piece of rope, about 12 feet long (depending on your tree)

3 small, heavy objects (like rocks, beanbags, or cans of food)

- Stick the tennis ball under one corner of the sheet, about 1 foot in.

- Place your open hand on top of the sheet, and pick up the tennis ball. Wrap your fingers around it tightly.

- With the help of an adult, use one end of the rope to tie a tight knot under the ball.

- Tie the other end of the rope around the trunk or a low branch of a tree. The ball should be about 4 feet off the ground.

- Gently pull the three free corners of the sheet away from the ball and the tree, forming a tent shape. This should also pull the ball gently away from the tree, although it will still be attached to the tree tightly by the rope.

- Hold the corners in place with your heavy objects.

190   HOW TO
HANG A PLAY TENT FROM TWO TREES

Flat bedsheet (the larger the better)

Piece of rope, at least 12 feet long (depending on the location of your trees)

4 small, heavy objects (like rocks, beanbags, or cans of food)

- Lay the sheet on the ground and fold it in half.

- With the help of an adult, find two trees that are roughly 6–12 feet apart.

- Tie one end of the rope around the trunk or a low branch of one tree.

- Tie the other end of the rope around the second tree at a similar height. It should hang horizontally, like a clothesline. Before you tighten the second knot, pull the rope hanging between the trees tighter or looser so that in the middle is 1½–2 feet lower than the height of the folded sheet.

- Drape the sheet over the rope along the fold.

- Pull the four corners out into a tent shape, and hold them in place with your heavy objects.

191   HOW TO
BUILD A HULA-HOOP HIDEOUT

2 flat twin-size bedsheets

Hula-Hoop

Duct tape

3 pieces of rope or twine, each about 4 feet long

- Lay one bedsheet out flat.
- Place the Hula-Hoop along the top (the short end), and fold it over 2–3 inches. Duct tape along the seam, moving the Hula-Hoop and sheet as you go to keep the Hula-Hoop inside the seam.

- Repeat with the second bedsheet so that both are attached to the Hula-Hoop.

- Tie one end of a piece of rope around the Hula-Hoop between the two sheets. Then tie the other two pieces of rope to the Hula-Hoop between the sheets on the other side.

- With the help of an adult, gather up the three free ends of the rope and secure the Hula-Hoop hideout to a tree, rafter, or other high spot.

192 HOW TO
PLAY ROCK-PAPER-SCISSORS

- Learn the three hand moves:

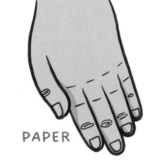

ROCK

PAPER

SCISSORS

- Have each player make a fist and hold it in front of them. Together say, "Rock, paper, scissors—shoot!" On "shoot," each of you should quickly form your hand into rock, paper, or scissors.

- See who won the round:

ROCK SMASHES SCISSORS

PAPER COVERS UP ROCK

SCISSORS CUT UP PAPER

IF PLAYERS FORM THE SAME HAND MOVE, IT'S A TIE. PLAY AGAIN.

Make up your own new hand moves and rules!

GRASS

SNAIL

HAWK

BUILD AN ARCHIMEDES SCREW

A screw is a simple machine. It has a long, inclined plane (like a ramp) wrapped around a pole or a cone. It can be used to hold things together or lift things—an Archimedes screw can even lift water!

> Thin, clear plastic tubing (about ¼-inch wide, about twice as long as the stick—can be purchased at a hardware store)
>
> Thick stick or branch (about 1-2 feet long)
>
> Clear packing tape
>
> Large bowl
>
> Food coloring
>
> Baking pan

Tape the bottom of the plastic tubing to the bottom of the stick.

Wrap the tubing around and around the stick toward the top. Tape every few times around to hold it in place.

Tape the top of the tubing in place at the top of the stick.

- Fill the bowl with water. Add a few drops of food coloring so that it will be easier to see.

- Place the bowl next to the baking pan. Place the Archimedes screw in the bowl.

- Hold the screw at an angle, tipped to the side over the baking pan. Slowly turn it, and watch what happens. Then turn it the other direction to see what happens.

194 HOW TO
FORM ANIMAL SHADOW PUPPETS

Make shadows with any part of your body! Use these ideas for hand shadows outdoors on a bright sunny day, or indoors by a lamp.

CRAB

CHEETAH

BABY BEAR

MOOSE

BIRD

SNAIL

2+

195 HOW TO
ACT LIKE AN ANIMAL

Scissors

A few sheets of paper

Drawing tools (colored pencils/pens, markers, or crayons)

Glass jar (that can be recycled)

- Cut the paper into pieces, each about the size of your hand. Start with at least 10.

- Draw a picture of an animal on each piece.

- Fold up each finished piece, and put it in the jar.

- Have one player pull a piece from the jar and secretly look at the animal. This player must act like this animal. They can make sounds, but they can't say any words.

- The other player (or players) must guess. The first player to guess correctly goes next.

STOMP LIKE A GIANT

2+

1 or more large cardboard boxes (the bigger the better)

Drawing tools (colored pencils/pens, markers, or crayons)

Scissors

Duct tape

2 empty rectangular tissue boxes for each player

- Unfold and flatten the large cardboard box.

- Find the largest area with no folds, and draw the shape of a large foot, about 2–3 feet long. (It could be a human foot, clawed animal foot, or a silly shape in between!)

- Cut it out.

- Trace the foot on another piece of cardboard, and cut it out so that you have two large feet.

- Decorate the feet.

- Use four or more large pieces of tape to securely attach a tissue box in the middle of each foot.

- Repeat the previous steps to make a second set of feet.

- Select starting and finish lines about 10 feet apart. Have each player step into their tissue boxes behind the starting line.

- Together count: "1, 2, 3, stomp!" Race to cross the finish line first to win.

Cut a toe hole in the tissue boxes to fit larger feet.

1, 2, 3, STOMP!

INCH LIKE A WORM

INCH LIKE A WORM:

- Stand with both feet together. While keeping your legs straight, bend down and place your hands on the floor in front of you.

- Slowly walk your hands: One at a time, move your hands forward on the floor until you are in a push-up position.

- Slowly walk your feet: One at a time, walk your feet toward your hands until you are in the starting position. Keep going!

WALK LIKE A CRAB:

- Sit on the floor with your knees bent in front of you. Place your hands on the floor behind you. Push up onto your hands and feet so that your bottom is off the floor.

- One at a time, pick up one hand and then one foot and step forward. Keep going!

HOP LIKE A FROG:

- Stand with both feet together. Bend your knees to squat down, placing your hands in front of you on the floor.

- Push off with your feet, straighten your legs, and hop forward. Land on your feet, and place your hands back in front of you. Keep going! (What can you jump over?)

Think of your favorite animal, and make up your own way to move.

WATCH WORMS

Empty 2-liter bottle

Scissors

1–2 handfuls of small rocks

3–4 cups of dirt

1 cup of sand (or sandy dirt)

½ cup or more of fruit or vegetable skins, leaves, and stems

2–10 worms (dig for these outdoors!)

Masking tape

Sheet of dark construction paper

- Throw the bottle cap away.
- With the help of an adult, cut around the bottle a few inches down from the top, and save this piece.
- Fill the bottom with rocks. (This is very important for water drainage.)
- Create a few layers, alternating dirt, sand, and fruit/vegetable scraps.
- Add a handful of water to the top. (If the dirt is very dry, add a little more.)
- Add the worms.
- Tape the top of the bottle in place.
- Wrap the paper around the bottle, and tape it in place.
- Store the worms in a dark place for a few days. Then take them out, remove the paper, and peek at your worms at work!

Add a little more water if the dirt feels dry. Watch them for up to 10 days, then release them back outdoors.

SCULPT WITH PAPER CLIPS

Pile of paper clips
(at least 10)

Piece of string about
as tall as you

- Hold a paper clip with the loops at the bottom. Bend one out to the right and the other out to the left.

- Stretch out each end of the paper clip to form a *W* shape. Or flip it over to form an *M* shape.

- Loop the middle of the string around the corner of a table or other high object, and tie a knot with the ends so that it is at least 2 feet off the ground. (You may want to place a book on top of the string to hold it in place.)

- Hang the paper clip *W* on the string as the base of your sculpture. (The knot of the string should hold right at the center of the *W*.)

- Fold more paper clips into *W*s or *M*s or other shapes.

- Hang and balance more paper clips on your sculpture. How tall and wide can you build?

200 HOW TO
CONNECT PAPER CLIPS
WITHOUT TOUCHING THEM

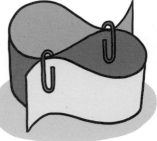

> Sheet of paper
> Scissors
> 2 paper clips

TIP: If your paper clips didn't "magically" connect, practice the trick again and pull the paper apart a little slower or a little faster.

- Cut a strip from the long side of the paper. It should be about as wide as the length of your finger.

- Fold the strip like an *S*, and attach two paper clips, as shown.

- Grab one end of the strip in each hand.

- You are ready for your trick: "1, 2, 3, magic!" Pull your hands quickly apart at the same time. Watch the paper clips do their magic trick.

201 HOW TO
BEND A PAPER CLIP HEART

> Paper clip
> Love note

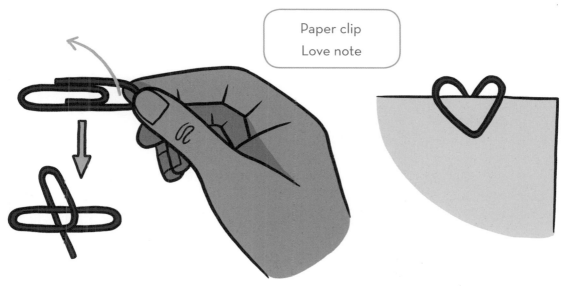

Hold the longest loop of a paper clip in your right hand. Bend the paper clip in the middle to push the long loop up.

Clip this middle bend of the paper clip over a note to hide the back portions of the paper clip, and form a heart.

MAKE MUSIC WITH SPOONS

2 metal spoons

- Make a fist with your strongest hand. Stick one spoon in between your pointer and middle fingers. Stick the other spoon in just below, between your middle and ring fingers. Turn the spoons so that their rounded backs face each other.

- To create sounds, loosen your hand a little as you quickly flap it up and down so that the backs of the spoons move up and down, hitting each other. Experiment until you get it just right—not too loose or too tight.

- To make a rhythm, gently slap the spoons against your other palm. Then use your knee, your leg, or something nearby. Gently slap between two objects to change the rhythm. Or sing or listen to music—tap and slap along with the songs.

FLIP A SPOON

2 spoons

Large plastic cup

- Lay the two spoons in a row, pointed at the cup like in the picture. Use your hand to slap down firmly on the top of the front spoon.

- Watch what happens. (If the second spoon doesn't flip into the cup, place the spoons closer or farther and try again.)

- How many times in a row can you land in the cup?

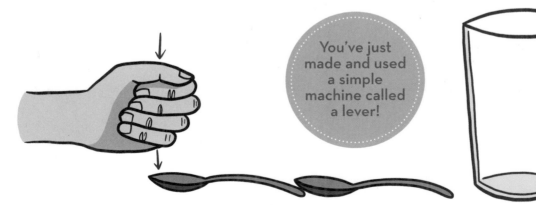

You've just made and used a simple machine called a lever!

MAKE A POM-POM

Scissors
Ball of yarn
Fork

Cut a piece of yarn about as long as your hand, and set it aside.

Take the yarn at the end of the yarn ball, and hold it against the tines of the fork. Wrap the ball of yarn around the fork two times to hold the end in place.

Continue wrapping tightly, about 20 more times. Keep the yarn in the middle of the tines.

Cut the end of the yarn, and hold it in place. Take the short piece of yarn you had set aside, thread it through the bottom of the fork tines, and tie a tight knot around the wrapped yarn.

Push all the yarn off the fork. Tighten the knot, and add another knot to make sure it's secure. With the help of an adult, carefully cut the loops of yarn to create the pom-pom's fringe. Trim any pieces that are too long.

205 HOW TO
MAKE YOUR OWN HOT COCOA MIX

1 cup of powdered sugar

½ cup of unsweetened cocoa powder

1 heaping cup of dry powdered milk

Pinch of salt

Large bowl and whisk

Airtight container
(like a jar with a lid)

Optional mix-ins: handful of mini marshmallows, 1 crushed candy cane, 2 spoonfuls of mini chocolate chips, 1 teaspoon of cinnamon

- Combine the ingredients in the bowl.

- Mix well with a whisk. Add in any optional mix-ins.

- Store the hot cocoa mix in an airtight container for up to six months.

To make a drink, add two heaping spoonfuls to a mug of warm or hot water. Stir and enjoy.

206 HOW TO
MAKE FROZEN HOT COCOA

1 packet of instant hot cocoa mix (or 1½ tablespoons of your own mix)

¾ cup of milk

1 cup of ice cubes

Blender

Drinking glass

Optional toppings: whipped cream, chocolate sprinkles, and chocolate syrup

- Pour the hot cocoa mix, milk, and ice cubes into your blender.

- Blend on high for 1 minute or until smooth.

- Pour your frozen hot cocoa into a glass. Add toppings and enjoy!

MAKE A HOT COCOA BROWNIE (IN A MUG!)

- 2 tablespoons of butter
- Mug
- 2 tablespoons of milk
- 1 tablespoon of brown sugar
- Spoon
- 1 packet of instant hot cocoa mix (or 1½ tablespoons of your own mix)
- ¼ cup of flour
- 1 tablespoon of chocolate chips
- Pinch of salt

- Place the butter in your mug, and microwave for 30 seconds or until melted.

- Add 2 tablespoons of water, milk, and brown sugar to your mug. Stir with a spoon until combined.

- Add hot cocoa mix, flour, chocolate chips, and salt. Stir again until well combined.

- Microwave for 90 seconds or until cooked through.

- Carefully remove the mug—it will be hot! Let the brownie cool for 1–2 minutes before enjoying.

This brownie fills the mug only halfway—leaving room for a scoop of ice cream on top!

MAKE HOT COCOA PANCAKES

- 1 cup of flour
- 1 tablespoon of sugar
- 1 packet of instant hot cocoa mix (or 1½ tablespoons of your own mix)
- 2 teaspoons of baking powder
- ½ teaspoon of salt
- Mixing bowl
- Spoon
- 1 cup of milk
- 3 spoonfuls of melted butter
- 1 large egg
- Nonstick skillet
- Spatula

- Add the flour, sugar, hot cocoa, baking powder, and salt to the bowl. Mix well with a spoon.

- Use the spoon to dig a well in the middle. Pour in the milk and 2 spoonfuls of melted butter. Crack in the egg.

- Using the spoon, stir the wet ingredients together. Then stir them into the dry ingredients around the outside. Continue stirring until they are mixed, but a few small lumps remain.

- With the help of an adult, heat the skillet on the stove to medium and add the last spoonful of butter.

- Pour a few small globs of batter onto the skillet to make small pancakes.

- Flip the pancakes when they are lightly browned.

- Remove the pancakes from the pan when they are cooked through.

Serve with chocolate sauce and whipped cream!

CUT A PAPER TRAIN CHAIN

Sheet of paper
Scissors
Clear tape
Pencil

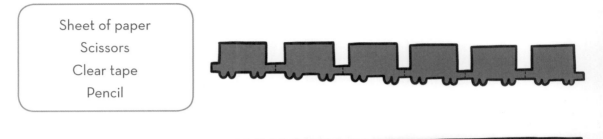

Fold the paper in half the long way.

Open it up, and cut along the fold line. You should have two long rectangles.

Lay them end to end, forming an even *longer* rectangle, and place a piece of clear tape across the entire joint.

Fold the long rectangle in half, along the tape joint. Then fold in the left side and the right side so that it is folded in equal thirds.

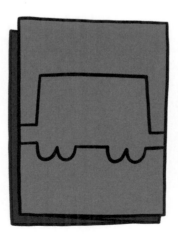

Make and add an engine and a caboose to your train.

Unfold the entire long rectangle. Use the fold lines to refold it into an accordion shape.

With the folds on the sides, draw your train car. Make sure to include a coupler on both sides that goes all the way to the edges of the folds. This needs to be at least as thick as your thumbprint. Cut it out.

HOW TO

MAKE A LAUGHING TRAIN

3+

- Have each player lie down to form a train, with their head on one other person's stomach.

- Take turns telling jokes. What happens when you laugh? Switch around the order and play again.

How can you know if the ocean is happy? See if it waves!

---

211 HOW TO

DRIVE THROUGH THE ALPHABET

2+

While in the car, work as a team to race through the alphabet.

- Start with the letter *A*. All players search outside the car on road signs, license plates, billboards, or buildings.

- The first player to spot the letter *A* points at it and announces, "I found A!" That player announces the next letter, *B*.

- All players work together to make it through the entire alphabet, all the way to *Z*. To play it competitively: Each player moves on to the next letter at their own pace. Whoever gets to *Z* first wins.

Q. How can you write the alphabet in 11 letters?

A. THE ALPHABET

MAKE A KALEIDOSCOPE

Permanent marker

Clear, thin plastic (at least as large as your open hand—like from the top of a fruit or bakery container)

Scissors

Ruler

Sheet of thick paper

Glue stick

Piece of foil (as large as your sheet of paper)

Clear tape

11-inch paper tube (from a paper towel roll or wrapping paper)

Handful of beads and/or sequins

- Trace around the end of the tube onto the clear plastic two times.

- Cut out one circle. Then cut *inside* the lines of the other circle, trimming so that the circle is small enough to fit inside the tube.

- Measure and cut three strips of paper that are each 10 inches long and 1¼ inches wide.

- Add glue to one side of each strip of paper, and glue them (without touching each other) to the duller side of the foil. Then cut them out. You should have three strips that are paper on one side and shiny foil on the other.

- Tape the strips together to form a long triangle with the foil on the *inside*.

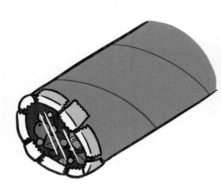

Stand the tube up on your work surface. Drop the foil triangle inside the tube. Put the smaller plastic circle on top of it, sitting inside the tube, and tape it in place with tape.

Add your beads and sequins, and leave enough room for them to move around. Place the larger plastic circle on top, like a lid, and tape it in place with clear tape.

Flip the tube over. Use small pieces of tape to cover the edges so that only a triangle shape remains.

Hold the kaleidoscope up to the light, look through the triangular hole, and spin it!

MAKE A PINWHEEL

Square piece of paper
(see page 8—any size will work)

Drawing tools (colored pencils/pens, markers, or crayons)

Cup

Scissors

Hammer

Small nail (around ¾ inch works well)

Wooden dowel (about 1 foot long) or chopstick

Bead (should fit on the nail)

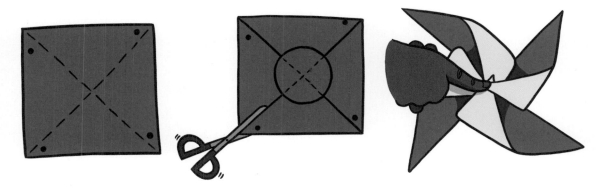

- Fold the square piece of paper in half diagonally. Unfold, and fold it in half the other way. Unfold again. You should have four triangles.

- Color and decorate the triangles on *both* sides of the paper.

- On one side, add a dot to the right corner of each of the four triangles.

- Place the cup upside down in the middle of the paper, and make a mark where it touches each of the four lines.

- Starting in each outside corner, use scissors to cut in on each fold line until you hit your mark.

- With the help of an adult, use the hammer to lightly tap your nail into the side of the top of the dowel. Then remove it, leaving a hole.

- Pull one dot of the pinwheel into the middle. Go around the circle, pulling all four to the middle.

- Gently push the nail through all four pieces, and keep pushing through the center of the paper (where the folds make an *X*).

- Add the bead to the back of the nail (behind all the papers), then push it into the hole in the dowel tightly. Blow to watch it spin!

WIN A TOSS-UP

Coin

- Hold one hand in a tight fist.

- Bend your thumb in half, and tuck it inside your top finger, the pointer finger.

- Place a coin flat on top—half on your thumb and half on your bent pointer finger.

- Press your thumbnail against your finger as hard as you can to pop it up. Watch the coin flip and fly.

IF IT'S HEADS—YOU WIN.

IF IT'S TAILS—FLIP AGAIN. THIS TIME YOU NEED *TWO* HEADS IN A ROW TO WIN.

- Each time you flip another tails, you need *another* heads in a row to win—three, then four, then more.

GRAB COINS OFF YOUR ELBOW

10 quarters

- Bend your elbow. Hold it up high, with your forearm parallel to the floor and your hand up near your shoulder, your palm facing up (toward your ear).

- Place one quarter on the top of your elbow.

- Very quickly snap your palm forward, and try to grab the coin before it falls.

- It takes practice, so snap (and snap and snap) again.

- Once you get it, add a second quarter, then a third, and more.

MAKE A COIN DISAPPEAR

Coin (a quarter works best because of its size)

TIP: Practice in front of a mirror until you can do the trick quickly and easily.

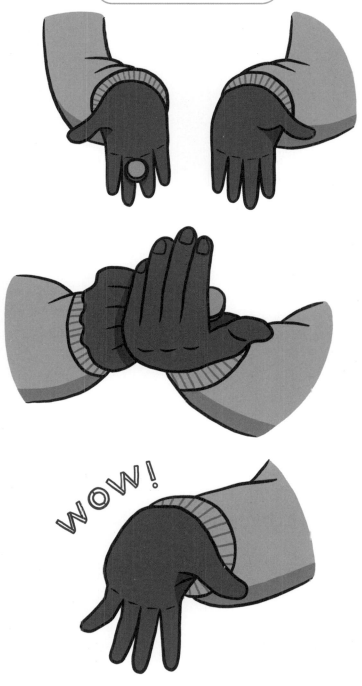

WOW!

- Hold both hands out in front of you. Place a coin on the middle two fingers of your right hand.

- Place your right thumb on top of the coin.

- Flip your hand over, and pretend to slap it into your left palm. (Here's the trick: You want to make it *look* like the coin is being slapped into your left hand, but really, your thumb holds it in your right hand.) So, as you get closer, curl the fingers on your left hand up to block the view. After the pretend transfer, keep your left hand closed, like it is holding the coin, and drop your right hand (still holding the coin) down to the you side, like it's done with its job.

- You are ready for your reveal: "1, 2, 3, magic!" Open your left hand, and wow your fans that your hand is empty.

- When you are ready to make the coin reappear, tap your right hand into your left hand and transfer the coin.

217   HOW TO
MAKE WASHABLE SIDEWALK PAINT

- In the medium bowl, use a paintbrush to mix the cornstarch with 1 cup of water until smooth.

- Pour the mixture evenly into four small bowls.

- Squeeze a dollop of a different colored paint into each bowl—about 1 tablespoon in each. (Mix the paints to create new colors, too!)

- Use one paintbrush for each color to mix each bowl. Then paint your own sidewalk art.

Medium bowl

4 paintbrushes

1 cup of cornstarch

4 small plastic bowls

Washable tempera paint (4 colors)

218   HOW TO
CREATE STAINED-GLASS CHALK ART

Masking tape (or painter's tape)

Sidewalk chalk

- Find a clean and smooth sidewalk or driveway, safe from traffic.

- Tear off long pieces of tape to mark out a large rectangle. (If you have room to make it as long as you, that's great!)

- Tear off more pieces of tape to divide up the inside of the rectangle with straight lines. Create squares, triangles, parallelograms, hexagons, and more.

- Use the chalk to fill in each shape with one color.

- Peel up the tape to reveal your stained-glass design!

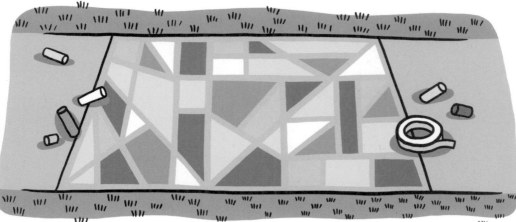

219 HOW TO
CREATE STAINED-GLASS CANDY

Baking tray

Parchment paper

Nonstick cooking spray

20 or more hard candies (in many colors)

Kitchen mallet (or any canned good)

Resealable plastic bag

- With the help of an adult, preheat the oven to 350°F.
- Line the baking tray with parchment paper. Coat with nonstick spray.
- Unwrap the candies, and place all of one color in the bag.
- Gently break the candy into pieces with the mallet.
- Dump the broken candies into a pile on the parchment paper.
- Repeat the steps for each color so you have a separate pile of each color on the parchment paper.
- Place piles of candy in the oven for 4–7 minutes, until they have fully melted into flat puddles. (They should not bubble—that can quickly lead to burning.)
- Remove the pan, and let it rest for 30 minutes or more, until fully cooled and hardened.
- Gently tap the hard candy with the mallet to break it into shards. Share and enjoy.

220 HOW TO
BUILD A CANDY TETRAHEDRON

A tetrahedron is a three-dimensional shape with four triangles making up the four sides.

4 or more gumdrops, small marshmallows, or jelly beans

6 or more toothpicks

① Press three toothpicks into three gumdrops to form a triangle.

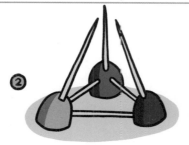

② Lay the triangle down. Press one toothpick into the top of each gumdrop, facing up.

③ Add the last gumdrop on top, connecting the last three toothpicks.

Keep adding to your structure with more gumdrops and more toothpicks!

BUILD A BEE HOTEL

Materials:

Bottle opener

Empty and clean metal can of any size

Piece of string about as tall as you

Lots of paper straws

Scissors

There are thousands of species of bees—some are called solitary bees because they don't live in hives. By using different sizes of straws, you may attract different sizes and species of solitary bees.

- Use the bottle opener to punch a small triangular hole in the closed end of the can.

- Thread the string through the can.

- Make the rooms: Place a paper straw inside. Use your fingers to mark the spot where you'll need to cut it so that it doesn't hang out the end of the can.

- Cut the straw. Then cut more straws the same length, and place them in the can until they are tightly packed enough to stay in place.

- Using the string, hang the bee hotel outdoors where it will not be disturbed.

- Check back in a few days and then a few weeks, or even a few months. You will know if any bees have laid eggs because they will use mud or other materials to make little doors. After the new bee hatches, it will fly away!

CATCH FRUIT FLIES

Tiny fruit flies like to eat sugary foods like ripe fruit. They are common in kitchens, especially in the warmer months. Make this simple contraption and you'll have some new pets!

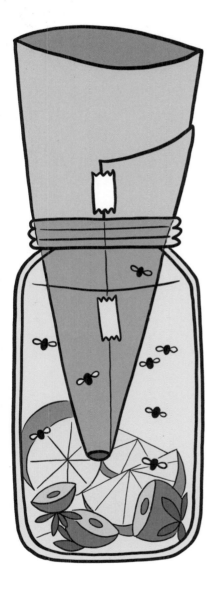

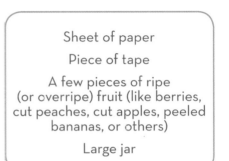

Sheet of paper

Piece of tape

A few pieces of ripe (or overripe) fruit (like berries, cut peaches, cut apples, peeled bananas, or others)

Large jar

- Roll the paper into a cone. Leave a hole in the bottom about the size of your finger.

- Tape the cone to hold the shape.

- Place a few pieces of fruit in the bottom of the jar.

- Place the cone in the jar. The outside of the cone should touch the edge of the jar's mouth, creating a seal. (If it does not, reroll the cone a little wider.)

- Wait overnight to see if you've caught any fruit flies. Release them outdoors by lifting out the paper cone.

PLANT AN AVOCADO SEED

The large pit in the middle of an avocado is a seed.

> Clean avocado pit
>
> 3 toothpicks
>
> Glass jar (can be recycled)

- Hold the pit in your hand, and turn the smaller end to the top.

- With the help of an adult, push three toothpicks in around the middle.

- Place the pit over the top of the jar, held up by the toothpicks.

- Fill the jar with water so that the bottom third or half of the pit is submerged.

- Replace the water in the jar every few days to keep the bottom part of the pit underwater. Watch for a stem and roots to grow. (It will take a few weeks, sometimes more than a month, to see changes.)

- Once the stem has leaves and is taller than your hand, cut it in half. (This removes the top half and all the leaves, but it will help the plant grow stronger.)

- In a few weeks, when the plant regrows its leaves, it is ready to be planted.

WIN A SEED-SPITTING COMPETITION

> Small handful of clean seeds from a watermelon, apple, orange, or winter squash

- Go outdoors, and take a deep breath.

- Place one seed on your tongue. (Don't swallow it!)

- Here's the secret for maximum distance: Tip your head back, and lean back.

- 3, 2, 1, SPIT! At the same time, quickly fling your body and head forward, blow out, and spit the seed. The extra force of your body flinging forward and air leaving your mouth will propel the seed forward.

MAKE COLORFUL SEED BALLS

> 3 sheets of same-color
> construction paper
>
> Large bowl
>
> Blender
>
> Strainer
>
> Handful of wildflower
> seeds
>
> Wire rack

- Tear the construction paper into small pieces and place them in the bowl.

- Fill the bowl with water until the paper is covered. Allow it to sit overnight.

- With the help of an adult, pull handfuls of the soggy paper out and place them in a blender. Add water to fill the blender 1–2 inches higher than the paper.

- Turn the blender on and off in slow bursts until the paper is broken down into pulp and looks like oatmeal.

TIP: THE BLENDER WILL WORK BEST WHEN IT IS ABOUT 1/3 FULL WITH PAPER. WORK WITH SMALL BATCHES OF PAPER, AND REPEAT UNTIL ALL YOUR PAPER IS BLENDED.

- Place the strainer in the empty bowl, and pour the pulp into the strainer. Press down to help the water drain out.

- Remove the strainer, and empty the bowl of water. Dump the pulp into the dry bowl.

- Pour the seeds into the pulp, and mix with your hands.

- Make a ball of the pulp and seed mixture, just smaller than a golf ball, and roll it in your hands. Squeeze out any extra water.

- Place the ball on the wire rack. Repeat until all the pulp is rolled up.

- Leave the seed balls to dry for several days.

- When they are dry, take the seed balls outdoors and throw them where you want to plant wildflowers. (Or you could give them as gifts!)

HOLLOW OUT AN EGG

> 2 or more eggs in a carton
> (white eggs work best)
>
> Sewing needle
>
> Toothpick
>
> Large bowl
>
> Optional: straw

- Wash the eggs with soap and water.

- With the help of an adult, use a sewing needle to poke a hole in one end of the first egg.

- Remove the needle, and carefully press in the toothpick to make the hole bigger.

- Move the toothpick in and out, and wiggle it for about a minute. Your goal is to poke the yolk inside the egg. Flip the egg so that the hole is over the bowl. Use the needle first, and the toothpick second, to make a matching hole in the top.

- While still holding the egg over the bowl, press your lips onto the top and blow into the hole. Blow until the yolk and white of the egg start to come out the bottom hole.

TIPS: If you don't want to put your lips on the egg, hold a straw over the hole and blow into the other end of the straw. Cutting it shorter can make it easier to work with. And if the insides of the egg won't come out, use the toothpick to make both holes larger.

- When all the insides are in the bowl, gently wash the egg.

- Repeat with the other eggs, and place them in the carton to dry overnight.

227 HOW TO
DECORATE AN EGG WITH WHIPPED CREAM

Spoon

Muffin tin

Whipped cream

Gel food coloring

Eggs (hollowed-out or hard-boiled—white eggs work best)

- Use a spoon to fill a cup of the muffin tin with whipped cream. (Fill another cup for each additional egg you want to decorate.)

- Add a few drops of different colors of food coloring to each cup.

- Use the handle end of the spoon to swirl the colors. (Be careful not to mix them all the way up.)

- Press an egg down into each cup, and leave it for 10 minutes.

- Pick up the eggs, and flip them over. Leave them for 10 minutes again.

- Remove the eggs, and rinse them.

228 HOW TO
PAINT KEEPSAKE EGGS

2 or more eggs in a carton (white eggs work best— hollowed-out, hard-boiled, or fresh)

Liquid watercolors (or food coloring)

4 or more paper straws

- Use four or more cradles of the egg carton as a paint palette: Fill the bottom half with one color of liquid watercolor each. (You can also mix colors or use food coloring mixed with a little bit of water.)

- Place an egg in an empty cradle.

- Dip a straw into one color, and press your thumb over the top.

- Lift up the straw, keeping your thumb pressed tightly. When you are over the egg, release your thumb and drizzle the color.

- Repeat with a fresh straw for each color until your egg is decorated.

- Repeat again with your other eggs, and leave them to dry overnight.

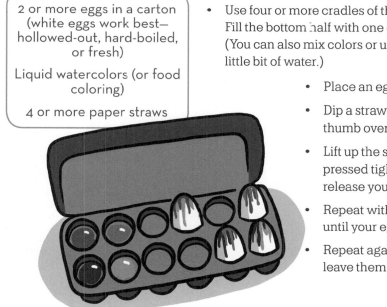

FOLD A NEWSPAPER CAP

| 1 full sheet of newspaper |

Start with the newspaper folded in half. Rotate the crease to the top.

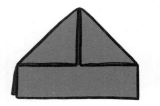

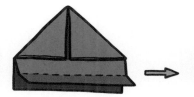

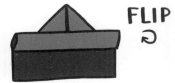

FLIP

Fold down the two top corners so that they meet evenly in the middle.

Fold up the front bottom flap with two folds: First fold it halfway up. Then fold it the rest of the way.

Flip the newspaper over to the back.

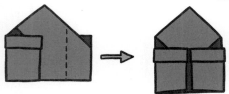

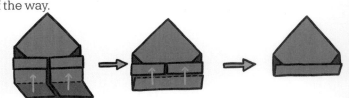

Fold in both sides to meet in the middle.

Fold up the bottom flap (which is two sheets thick) in two folds: First fold it halfway up. Then fold it the rest of the way.

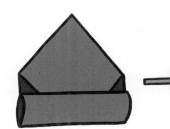

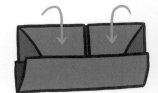

Unfold it halfway, and tuck the top of the flap into the band of the hat. Fold the top of the hat all the way down, and tuck it into the same band of the hat.

Use the same instructions to fold a doll-sized cap from a sheet of regular paper!

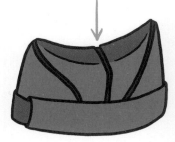

Open up the hat from the bottom, and press down the center of the top to form the shape.

FOLD A GIANT NEWSPAPER HAT

1 full sheet of newspaper

1 **2**

- Start with the newspaper folded in half. Rotate the crease to the top.

- Fold down the two top corners so that they meet evenly in the middle.

- Fold up the front bottom flap.

- Flip it over, and fold up the back bottom flap.

3 FLIP **4**

TALK LIKE A PIRATE

Avast ye! No time to make up a secret language? Talk to your friends like pirates—all hands on deck!

AHOY, MATEY
Hi, friend.

We need everyone's help!
ALL HANDS ON DECK!

Oh my!
SHIVER ME TIMBERS

getting used to being on the water
SEA LEGS

Check this out.
AVAST YE

to trick someone
HORNSWOGGLE

POOP DECK
top back deck of a boat

THAR SHE BLOWS!
I see something!

BATTEN DOWN THE HATCHES
Get ready for a storm (or another event).

BOOTY
treasure

Rats!
BLIMEY!

Work hard!
HEAVE-HO!

person who doesn't understand life on the water
LANDLUBBER

clean (or under control)
SHIPSHAPE

MAKE CRISPY SPRINKLE TREATS

- 2 ounces of chocolate (white, milk, or dark)
- ½ cup of peanut butter (or a nut-free alternative)
- 2 tablespoons of honey
- Large microwave-safe bowl
- Spoon
- 2 cups of puffed rice cereal
- 6 cupcake wrappers
- Muffin tin
- Sprinkles

- With the help of an adult, place the chocolate, peanut butter, and honey into the bowl and microwave for 30 seconds.

- Carefully remove the bowl, and stir. Repeat, microwaving for 8–10 seconds at a time and stirring again until the mixture is melted.

- Add the puffed rice cereal to the bowl, and stir until combined.

- Place the cupcake wrappers in the muffin tin, and use the spoon to fill each one. Press down with the spoon until each wrapper is tightly packed.

- Add sprinkles on top.

- Place the treats in the refrigerator for 30 minutes, or until chilled.

BAKE A COOKIE PUZZLE

- Baking tray
- Parchment paper
- 1 package of premade sugar cookie dough (about 16 ounces)
- Rolling pin
- Cutting board and knife
- Cookie cutters
- Wire rack
- 1 cup of powdered sugar
- 2 tablespoons of milk
- Small bowl
- Spoon
- Sprinkles

- Line the baking tray with parchment paper.

- Place the cookie dough on top, and roll out a rectangle about ¼-inch thick.

- With the help of an adult, bake according to the package instructions.

- When the cookie is done, remove it from the oven and carefully lift the parchment paper and dough onto the cutting board.

- Immediately use cookie cutters and a knife to cut the still-soft dough into shapes and pieces.

- Carefully separate each piece, and place them on the wire rack until cool.

- Place sugar and milk in the bowl, and mix well with a spoon.

- When the cookies are cool, place a spoonful of thin frosting on each piece and use the back of the spoon to spread it around.

- Add sprinkles.

- Solve the puzzle—and eat!

BAKE MINI PIE POCKETS

Baking tray

Parchment paper

Package of premade rolled pie crusts (about 12–20 ounces)

Cutting board and knife

Index card (or other piece of paper of similar size)

Jam or jelly (1 or more flavors)

Fork and spoon

Wire rack

1 cup of powdered sugar

1 tablespoon of milk

Small bowl

Sprinkles

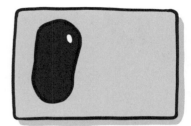

- With the help of an adult, preheat your oven to 400°F.

- Line the baking tray with parchment paper.

- Thaw the pie crusts according to the package instructions, then spread them out on the cutting board. Use the index card as an outline to cut the crust into rectangles.

- Place one spoonful of jam on one half of each rectangle.

- Wet your finger with water, and trace along the outside edges of the rectangle.

- Fold the rectangles in half with the jam inside.

- Press the fork around the edges to close each pocket. Flip each pocket over, and repeat on the other side.

- Bake for 14–16 minutes or until lightly browned and cooked through. Set on the wire rack for 10 minutes, or until cool.

- Mix the powdered sugar and milk in the small bowl. Stir in one spoonful of jam to make the frosting.

- Apply the frosting to the top of each pocket with the spoon. Add sprinkles. Share and enjoy.

Use cookie cutters to make pockets of different shapes!

PLAY BOCCE IN YOUR BACKYARD

Bocce is a sport that has been played for hundreds of years. Play your own version outdoors—score 3 points to win!

> Small ball (like a baseball, tennis ball, or golf ball)
>
> 4 different, ideally larger, balls for each player (for example: rubber balls, softballs, or beach balls)

- Select an area outdoors that is flat and grassy. Mark a pitch line that players will not cross (this could be a driveway or a stick to stand behind).

- One player should take the small ball, called the jack, and toss it several feet (or several yards) away in the grass.

- Players take turns tossing their larger balls, trying to get as close as possible to the jack.

> HITTING THE JACK TO MOVE IT IS AN OKAY STRATEGY.
>
> HITTING ANOTHER PLAYER'S BALL TO MOVE IT IS AN OKAY STRATEGY.

- When all the balls have been thrown, score the round:

> LOOK AT THE CLOSEST BALL TO THE JACK— IT IS WORTH 1 POINT. (IF IT IS ACTUALLY TOUCHING THE JACK—IT IS WORTH 2 POINTS.)
>
> IF THE NEXT CLOSEST BALL BELONGS TO THE SAME PLAYER, ANOTHER POINT IS EARNED.
>
> THE SCORING STOPS WHEN THE NEXT CLOSEST BALL BELONGS TO A DIFFERENT PLAYER.
>
> A GAME OF BOCCE ENDS WHEN ONE PLAYER REACHES 3 POINTS.

236 HOW TO
PLAY FRISBEE GOLF

Frisbee golf uses a Frisbee instead of a golf ball, and goals instead of holes, but the rules are the same: Score the lowest number of points to win.

> Objects to make goals (like plastic cones, pinecones, sidewalk chalk, or other outdoor toys)
>
> Frisbee for each player (or for each team)
>
> Paper and pencil

- Play this game outdoors. Select the number and location of goals. Use objects around you (like chairs or trees) or objects you gather (like plastic cones or other outdoor toys) to agree on goals, and spread them out.

- Select a player to go first. This player throws their Frisbee and aims to *touch* the first goal. If they miss, they must throw again until they make it, counting all their throws.

- Take turns having the other players each aim at the first goal, counting their throws.

- When everyone is done, record the scores.

- Continue playing, aiming at the second goal, and then the others. When the game is over, the player with the lowest score, or least number of throws, wins.

237 HOW TO
PLAY ROLLING DARTS

PLAY INDOORS:
Use masking tape or string to make circles on the floor.

PLAY OUTDOORS:
Use Hula-Hoops, jump ropes, or sidewalk chalk to make circles on the ground.

- Make some circles overlap. Make some circles concentric—one inside the other. Make a starting line, too.

- Decide how many points each circle is worth.

- Stand behind the starting line.

- Roll a ball, and aim to get it inside the circles. How many points can you score?

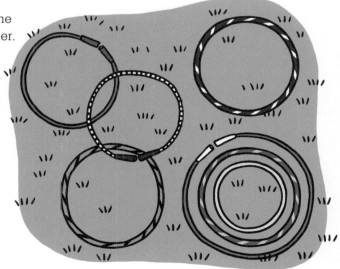

165

MAKE "OPENING A"

You can play many games by yourself or with a friend using just a piece of string. A common starting point is *"opening A."* Master this and you'll be ready for harder challenges.

> Loop of string (Take a piece of string or yarn that is about 48 inches long. Tie a knot with the ends to form a loop.)

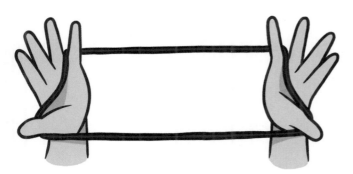

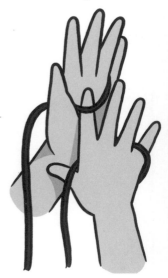

Begin with the string looped around your two pinkies. Scoop in your thumbs so that the string stretches across the inside of your other fingers. This is called the *"starting position."*

Keep your fingers straight up so that the string doesn't fall off. Move your right hand toward your left hand. Use your right pointer finger to scoop the loop from the center of your left hand.

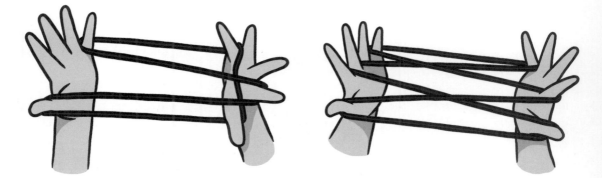

Pull your hands apart.

Do the same scoop with your other hand: Move your left hand over to your right. Use your left pointer finger to scoop the loop right in front of your right pointer finger.

Pull your hands apart to form *"opening A."*

239 HOW TO
MAKE CAT'S WHISKERS

"Cat's whiskers" is a game that uses a piece of string to create an interesting shape.

> Loop of string (Take a piece of string or yarn that is about 48 inches long. Tie a knot with the ends to form a loop.)

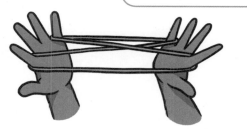

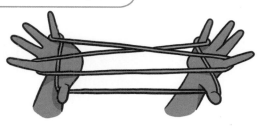

Begin with your loop of string in the *"opening A"* position. Lower your thumbs and drop both loops. The string should only be looped around your two pointer and pinkie fingers now.

Reach your thumbs under and allllll the way back to the string farthest away, the one looped around your pinkie. Grab it with your thumbs, and pull it back under.

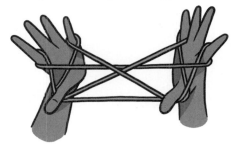

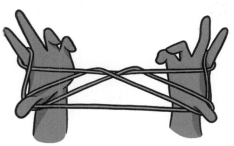

Now your thumbs will grab again: Reach over the closest string, and grab the second strings. Pull them back. (There will now be two strings looped around each thumb.)

Lower your pinkies, and drop both pinkie loops.

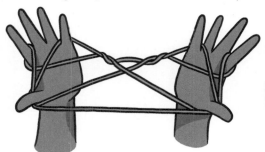

Reach your pinkies over the closest string, and grab the second strings. Pull them back.

Lower your thumbs, and drop both loops to form *"cat's whiskers."*

MAKE JACOB'S LADDER

"Jacob's ladder" is another game that uses a piece of string to create an interesting shape.

Loop of string
(Take a piece of string or yarn that is about 48 inches long. Tie a knot with the ends to form a loop.)

Begin with your loop of string in "*cat's whiskers.*" With both thumbs, reach over the closest two strings and grab the third strings. Pull them back.

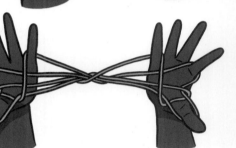

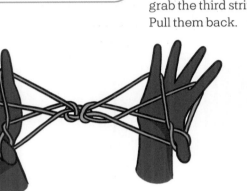

Reach your right thumb up to touch the base of your right pointer finger. Slide it under the loop, and scoop it back.

You should now have two loops on your right thumb. (To make it easier, use your left hand to help move the loop onto your right thumb.)

Do the same thing with your left hand. (Again, use your right hand to help move the loop onto your left thumb.)

Move your right hand toward your left hand. Pull the bottom loop off your left thumb, and release it. Do the same thing with your left hand. (There should now be one loop around each thumb.)

Stick both pointer fingers down into the small triangles right by your thumbs.

Lower your pinkies, and let the loops fall off.

Push your pointer fingers deeper into the triangles. The old loops on both of your pointer fingers will fall off as you turn your palms away from you, forming "*Jacob's ladder.*"

MAKE A YARN DOLL

Scissors

Ball of yarn

Small thin book
(it should be the height you
want your doll to be)

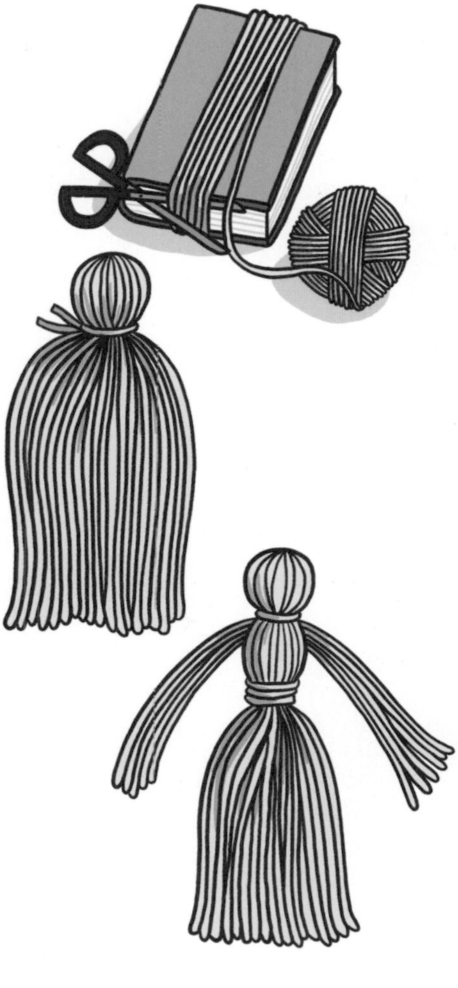

- Cut five pieces of yarn from the ball. Each should be about as tall as the book. Set these aside.

- Hold one end of the string at the bottom of the book, and wrap around the tallest part. Keep wrapping about 25 times or so.

- With the help of an adult, cut across the bottom through all the yarn so you have one even cluster of pieces.

- Pull the cluster off the book so that it is still folded in half at the top. Tie one of the five extra pieces of yarn around the top, making a head for your doll.

- Separate about 10 pieces off to the right and 10 pieces off to the left. These will be your arms.

- Tie one or more strings around the yarn remaining in the middle—this becomes the body of your doll.

- To finish the arms, braid them or cut each arm shorter and then tie with a piece of yarn.

- To finish the body, leave the yarn as it is, like a dress, or separate and tie it to form two legs, like pants.

PLAY PONY EXPRESS

The Pony Express was a way of delivering mail in the United States more than 150 years ago. Riders on horseback carried mail between relay points over long distances. In this game, move fast enough to keep *all* your mail and capture some from the other team.

Paper

Drawing tools (colored pencils/ pens, markers, or crayons)

- Begin by having each player find a piece of paper. This will be your mail for the game. Each player should write or draw a picture, story, or letter on their mail.

- Divide the players into two teams.

- Select a course outdoors: It should take half a minute or more to run all the way around. (Running a loop from one tree to another and back works well.)

- Have one team stand in a row at the starting line. Have the other team stand in a row at the middle of the course. All players hold their letters.

- Together count,:"1, 2, 3, Pony Express!" The first player in each line should start running the same direction around the course.

For a challenge, gallop instead of run. Or use broomsticks as horses. Or run only on your tiptoes, or backward.

IF YOU RUN ALL THE WAY AROUND AND GET YOUR MAIL BACK TO WHERE YOU STARTED, YOU HAND IT TO THE NEXT PLAYER. THEY NOW HAVE TWO LETTERS AND START RUNNING.

IF YOU RUN FAST AND TAG THE OTHER PLAYER ON THE COURSE, YOU GET TO KEEP YOUR MAIL *AND* ALL THEIRS.

- Continue playing until each player has finished the course. The team with the most mail wins. Read the mail and then play again.

PLAY HORSE

Horse is a game about imagination and wild throws.

A ball and basket:

Outdoors—a basketball and hoop, a soccer ball and net, etc.

Indoors—a rolled-up sock and laundry hamper, a small stuffed animal and basket, etc.

The youngest player goes first. This player takes the ball and makes up a silly way to get it into the basket: They can stand on one leg and toss it with their eyes closed, they can make a fish face and throw it underhand, or they can spin around two times and fling it. (The shot *must go in* or the next player gets a turn to make up a silly shot.)

The next player must copy them *exactly* and aim the ball at the basket.

IF THE BALL GOES IN, THEN THE NEXT PLAYER TAKES THE SHOT.

IF THE BALL DOES NOT GO IN, THIS PLAYER EARNS THE FIRST LETTER OF HORSE: H.

When all the players have had a turn with the first shot, the first player makes another, different, silly shot. Each player must copy the new shot.

If the first player ever misses their shot, then it becomes the next player's turn to make up a silly shot.

Play continues as players make and miss shots. When a player misses five times and spells HORSE, they are out of the game. The last player left in the game wins.

FOLD A DDAKJI TILE

Ddakji is a folded-paper flipping game from South Korea. Make, decorate, and collect your own tiles.

> 2 pieces of square paper
> (see page 8—any size will work)
>
> Drawing tools (colored pencils/
> pens, markers, or crayons)

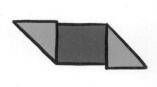

1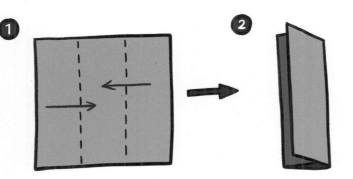

2

Fold each piece of paper into thirds: Fold in one side first, then the other side on top of it.

3

Fold in the opposite corners of each paper.

4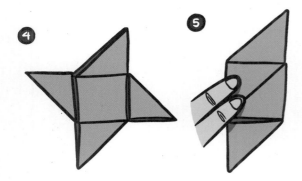

Stack them.

5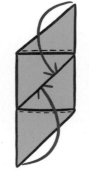

Fold in the side flaps.

Fold the bottom flap up and under the left flap. Fold the top flap down and under the right flap.

6

Decorate your tile with drawing tools.

245 HOW TO
PLAY DDAKJI

Earn points by throwing one tile from your hand at one on the ground to flip it over.

2 or more Ddakji tiles

- All the players stand. Choose one player to go first as the thrower. One tile is placed on the ground—a hard surface works best.

- The thrower holds the other tile. He throws it at the tile on the ground. The goal is to flip the ground tile over to score a point.

- Each player takes a turn being the thrower to see who can earn the most points.

TIP: Throw the tile down hard. Or see what happens when you aim at different places: the middle of the tile on the ground, or on the side, or corner.

246 HOW TO
PLAY TAPATAN

Line up three game pieces in a row to win.

Paper and pencil

3 matching game pieces for each player (these can be coins, cereal, paper clips, stones, or any small objects)

- Start by drawing the game board on a sheet of paper.
- Choose a player to go first. Take turns placing one game piece at a time on any dot on the board.

- The goal of the game is to get three of your game pieces in row. If all six pieces have been placed and no one has three in a row, take turns moving one of your own pieces along a line in any direction to the next dot. (No jumping allowed.)

- The first player to position three in a row wins the round. If the game gets stuck where neither player can move a piece, then the round is a tie.

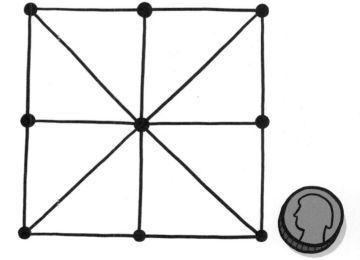

MAKE THE BRIGHTEST PAPER RAINBOW

Sheet of construction paper (any color)

Scissors

3 or more sheets of tissue paper (in different colors)

Pencil with an eraser

Bottle of school glue

Piece of foil

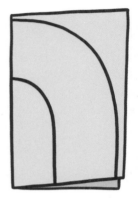

- Fold the top of the paper down to fold it in half.

- Turn the fold so that it is on your left, and draw half of a rainbow. It should start at the fold and extend down to the bottom of the paper on the right.

- Cut it out, and open it up.

- Count how many colors of tissue paper you have. Then use your pencil to divide the rainbow into that many stripes. (3–5 often works best—more than 5 can be hard to fit.)

- Cut the tissue paper into small squares, about 1 inch each. Start with about 20 of each color. (Cut more if you run out.)

- Squeeze a small pile of glue, about the size of a quarter, onto the foil. (Add more glue if you run out.)

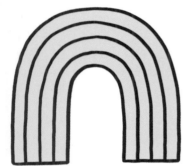

- Choose one color for the top stripe. Take a piece of tissue paper in your chosen color, and wrap it over the eraser of your pencil.

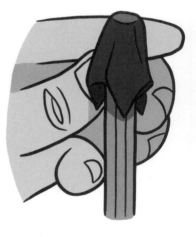

- Dip the eraser, still covered in the tissue paper, into the glue. Then, still holding the tissue paper on top of the eraser, press the tissue paper down on the stripe.

- Pull the pencil out, and repeat with a new piece of tissue paper. Use a different color for each stripe of the rainbow until it is complete.

MAKE A POP-UP RAINBOW CARD

Sheet of white paper

Small bowl

Drawing tools (colored pencils/ pens, markers, or crayons)

Scissors

Glue stick

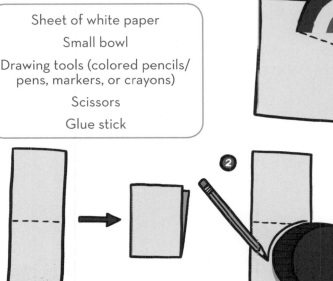

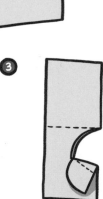

1 Fold the paper in half the long way, making a tall rectangle. Then fold it in half again, into quarters. Unfold it once, back to the long rectangle, with the fold on your right.

2 Place the small bowl upside down on the paper. It should be on the fold, just under the crease line. Trace *half* of the arc, like in the picture.

3 Cut on the arc line. Then fold it back. Make sure to leave a triangular shape against the fold. (This step is very important—it is necessary for the rainbow to pop up.)

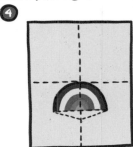

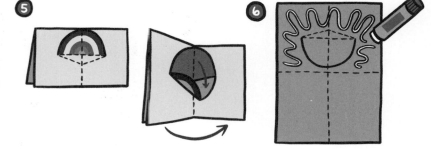

4 Open up the paper. Draw and color a rainbow on the cut-out arc shape.

5 Fold the paper in half with the rainbow on top. Push the rainbow forward, and fold in half again into a card shape—press down firmly to fold the rainbow forward.

6 Open the paper all the way up. On the back, add a layer of glue all over the rainbow half—but don't add any glue to the back of the rainbow. Fold the paper closed, and press down on the glue. Last, add a written message inside the card.

WALK THROUGH A SHEET OF PAPER

Sheet of paper
Pencil
Scissors

Before this magic trick, fold the paper in half the long way, making a tall rectangle. Use a pencil to lightly draw lines coming in from both sides like this:

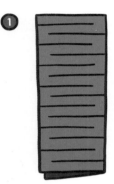

1

Each line should be spaced about the width of a finger from the next line and should *not* go all the way across to the other side.

Gather your audience, and show them the full, *unfolded* sheet of paper. (Hide the lines you drew on the back side.) "Get ready to be amazed! With my magic, I will now cut holes in this sheet of paper so that I can *walk right through it.*"

2

3

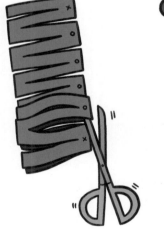

Fold the paper again, and cut along the lines, through both halves.

Then find the U-shaped loops along the fold side. Skip the first one on each end, but cut the remaining loops in the middle.

Stretch out the paper into a large ring and *walk right through!*

250 HOW TO
ALWAYS ROLL A 7 WITH ONE DIE

1 die

- Roll one die.

- Add up the numbers on the top and the bottom.

- Roll, and add again. Did you still get 7? Roll again. And again. (Guess what? The numbers always add up to 7.)

251 HOW TO
HEAR THROUGH A WALL

2+

Drinking glass

Sound vibrations travel better through solids, like the wall, than air.

- Have a friend or two go into another room. It must be next door to the room you are in and share a wall. Ask them to close the door and start talking.

- Place the bottom of your glass against the shared wall. Place your ear against the opening of the glass, and listen.

- Experiment with different spots on the wall until you find one that works best to hear.

252 HOW TO
PLAY KICKBALL KING

Keep your ball in the game the longest to win.

> Objects to define the playing space (plastic cones, pinecones, sidewalk chalk, or other outdoor toys)
>
> 1 large kicking ball for each player (soccer ball, rubber ball, beach ball, or similar)

Play indoors with balloons!

- Define a playing space. It should be about 10 feet or so across and any length—large enough for all the players to freely move around. Mark the edges with plastic cones or natural objects, like pinecones. Or use sidewalk chalk or objects already in the area, like a sidewalk or tree.

- Have all the players begin together somewhere inside the playing space with their balls—"Ready, set, go!"

- Each player starts running. The goal of the game is to protect your ball by keeping it inside the playing space *and* to kick other players' balls outside the playing space.

- When a player's ball is kicked out, they are out of that round. The last player with a ball inside the playing space wins.

253 HOW TO
PLAY TOWER TOPPLER

> Stack of paper cups
> Stack of index cards

- Set up the game: Lay one cup upside down on a table. Place an index card on top.

- Repeat this step until the tower of cups and index cards is five cups high. Then create another identical tower.

- Play the game: Have each player stand behind a tower. Together, say, "Ready, set, go!" Use your fingers to yank or flick the cards out of the tower *without* touching the cups.

- The first player to have all five cups tightly stacked wins.

- Play again with higher towers!

BUILD A CARD TOWER

Deck of cards

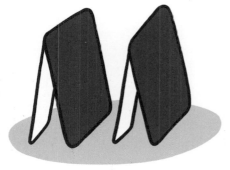

Balance two cards against each other to form a triangle. Next to the first triangle, balance a second triangle.

Carefully place a card on top to make one level.

Choose a solid place to build, like the floor or a table that doesn't wobble. At first, build on carpet or a place mat—the texture can help hold your cards in place.

To build higher, balance a two-card triangle on top.

To build wider (and then higher), make another triangle next to the first two, and place another card on top to make the level wider. Then build up again.

255 HOW TO
DRAW A ROAD TO NOWHERE

Drawing tools (colored pencils/
pens, markers, or crayons)

Sheet of paper (or a notebook)

1

Draw a road. It should start wide across the bottom of the paper and get smaller in the middle of the paper. (Like a wave shape.)

2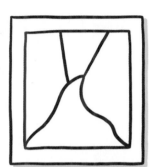

Draw two lines, each reaching from one top of the road to the top of the paper.

3

Fill both sides with more vertical lines. Make the lines in the middle, by the top of the road, close together. The lines by the sides of the paper can be farther apart.

4

Fill the middle section with horizontal lines.

5

Add a dashed line in the middle of the road. Color your design.

256 HOW TO
PLAY SQUIGGLE

Drawing tools (colored pencils/pens, markers, or crayons)

Few sheets of paper (or 2 notebooks)

- Each person starts by drawing a squiggle, any squiggle, on a sheet of paper or a page of a notebook.

- Swap squiggles.

- The goal is to draw an inventive and interesting drawing from your partner's squiggle.

Play by yourself: Close your eyes, and draw a squiggle. Then open your eyes, and get to work.

257 HOW TO
MAKE A FLIP-BOOK

Self-stick notepad

Drawing tools (colored pencils/pens, markers, or crayons)

- On the first page of the self-stick notepad, draw a simple shape.

- On the second page, draw the same object, but move it up, down, or over a little.

- On the third page, draw the same object again, but move it up, down, or over a little more.

- Finish 10–20 more pages. Then hold the spine, and quickly flip through the pages of your book to watch your drawing move.

Ready for something more complicated?

Draw a ball bouncing up and down.

Start with an empty pot, and slowly draw a plant growing in it.

Draw a basic monster, and add features growing on it. Hair! More eyes! Warts!

Start with one color, and slowly change it to another color.

258 HOW TO
SHOOT A MARBLE

> 1 marble

- Start with the hand you would use to hold a pencil, and make a fist.

- Tuck in your thumb so that your knuckle is held tight, right behind the knuckle of your pointer finger.

- Stick your pointer finger out straight. Your thumb shouldn't move—your middle finger should be holding it tightly in place.

- Place your marble at the top of your thumb and middle finger, and wrap your pointer finger back around it. (The tighter you hold it, the more power and accuracy your shot will have.)

- Rest your hand on a hard surface, such that any *one* of your knuckles is touching down.

- Now for the shot: Aim where you want the marble to go. Then hold your hand still, kick your thumb out, and watch the marble fly.

Master this marble skill to be the one to beat in any game of marbles!

259 HOW TO
SHOOT A MARBLE WITH BACKSPIN

> 1 marble

- Start with mastering How to Shoot a Marble.

- Now, make some adjustments to create the backspin:

  - Place your pinkie knuckle on the ground. Tip your hand so that the back of your hand is closer to the ground.

  - Lift your bent pointer finger a little.

- Straighten your thumb a little so that it is *under* the marble more.

- Move your thumb a little to one side or the other so that the marble is touching one side of your knuckle instead of the middle.

- Continue with your shot by aiming your marble and kicking your thumb out.

TIP: Learning to backspin a marble takes a lot of practice!
If you *don't* see a spin, make some tweaks:
Tip your hand a little bit forward or backward.
Put your thumb on the other side of the bottom of the marble.
Push the marble a little higher on your knuckle.

260 HOW TO
PLAY MARBLES

Use your shooter marble to knock other marbles out of the playing ring—more marbles mean more points!

> 13 marbles
>
> Shooter marble for each player (these can be the same size or larger than the playing marbles)
>
> Tools to draw a ring (a stick or chalk outdoors, masking tape or string indoors)

- Create a ring: This can be any size you want. To start, make it about 3 feet across. (In official games, this ring can be as big as 10 feet across!)

OUTDOORS, USE A STICK TO DRAW IN THE DIRT OR CHALK TO DRAW ON A HARDER SURFACE.

INDOORS, LAY OUT MASKING TAPE OR STRING ON THE FLOOR.

- Line up the 13 marbles in the shape of a cross in the middle.

- Choose a player to go first. You both must start outside the ring. Place your shooter marble anywhere on the outside. Follow the instructions, and shoot your marble into the ring.

    - If you knock any marbles out of the ring, you win them as points.
    - If your shooter stayed inside the ring, go again. Shoot from wherever your shooter is.
    - If your shooter rolled outside the ring, your turn is over.
    - If you do not knock any marbles out of the ring, you do not earn any points.
    - If your shooter stayed in, leave it where it is for your next turn.
    - If your shooter rolled out, pick it up. On your next turn, shoot from wherever you want outside the ring.

> If you shoot another player's shooter outside the circle, you win all their marbles (and points).

- Take turns and keep shooting marbles. When all 13 are out, whoever has the most wins.

261 HOW TO
PASS AN ORANGE WITH YOUR FEET

> Seat for each person
>
> 2 oranges (apples or small balls will also work)

- Have each person sit in a chair (or on a couch) in a row.

- The first person places the orange between their feet so it's being held tightly in place.

- Then this person must pass the orange to the next person, who must pass it to the next person, and so on. The trick is that no one is allowed to use their hands *or* arms.

- If the orange drops, it must be restarted with the first person.

- Practice again and again to see how fast you can pass it.

- If you have enough people, divide into two teams for a race.

Play the game again using only your elbows to pass the orange.

TIP: Place the orange on top of your feet so you can roll it off the side of your ankle to the next person. Or cross your ankles to make a safe basket for the orange to rest in.

262 HOW TO
MAKE AN ORANGE SLUSHIE

> 4 cups of orange juice (the juice of about 12 oranges)
>
> ¼ cup of honey
>
> 8-by-8-inch baking pan
>
> Fork
>
> Small bowls

- Place the orange juice and honey in the baking pan, and mix well with the fork.

- Place it in the freezer for 1 hour or more.

- Use the fork to scrape the orange juice mixture into pieces.

- Place it back in the freezer for 1 hour or more.

- Use the fork *again* to scrape the orange juice mixture into even smaller pieces.

- Scoop the slushie into small bowls, and enjoy, or repeat the scraping step one or more times, breaking the mixture into smaller pieces each time. Your slushie should have a snowlike texture.

Make a slushie with any liquid—cranberry juice, mango juice, or coconut milk!

263 HOW TO
MAKE FROZEN BANANA BITES

Baking tray

Parchment paper

1 cup of chocolate chips (or white chocolate chips)

Microwave-safe bowl

Spoon and fork

2 bananas (cut into about 20 small, round slices)

Optional: airtight container

- Line the baking tray with parchment paper.
- Place the chocolate chips into the bowl, and microwave for 30 seconds on high. Stir.
- Repeat microwaving and stirring until the chocolate is melted. (This usually takes about four rounds, or 2 minutes. Stirring often will help prevent the chocolate from burning.)
- Use a fork to fully dip a banana slice into the chocolate, and allow any extra to drip off. Place the banana on the parchment paper.
- Repeat with the rest of the banana slices.
- Place the baking pan of bananas into the freezer for 1 hour. Share and enjoy. (Or store the frozen bites in an airtight container in the freezer for up to 3 months.)

264 HOW TO
MAKE TWO-INGREDIENT BANANA ICE CREAM

Ripe banana

Bowl

Plastic wrap

Blender

3 tablespoons of milk (dairy or nondairy)

Spatula

- Peel the banana, and break it into about 10 small pieces.
- Place it in a bowl, and cover with plastic wrap. Freeze overnight.
- Place the banana pieces in a blender with the milk.
- Blend until creamy, like soft-serve ice cream. (If the mixture is too thick, add a bit more milk.)
- Use the spatula to move the banana ice cream back to the bowl. Eat it right away or re-cover it with plastic wrap and freeze for 1–2 hours for a firmer texture.

Break the two-ingredient rule and add a spoonful of nut butter, chocolate sauce, or dried fruit to the blender with the frozen banana pieces.

265 HOW TO
CRAFT A NATURE NAME

Natural materials (like rocks, leaves, pinecones, acorns, flowers and petals, grasses, seeds, pieces of bark, feathers, shells, or small sticks)

Plastic bucket or bowl

Sheet of paper

Glue (bottle or stick)

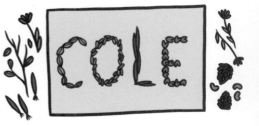

- Go on a nature walk. In the bucket, collect small items for your project.

- Experiment with your nature items on the paper. Lay them out to create lines and shapes. Stack and layer the items to create letters. Create the letters of your name.

- When you have spelled your name, add glue to the paper and attach each piece.

266 HOW TO
MAKE A DAISY CHAIN

10 or more daisies
(or other small flowers)

- Shorten the stems of the flowers by breaking off the ends. They should be a little longer than your hand, about 4 inches, but it doesn't have to be exact.

- Use your fingernail to make a small slit in the *middle* of each stem.

- Hold one flower in each hand. Push the stem of one flower through the slit in the other. Push it all the way through, until the daisy is touching the slit.

- Pick up another daisy, and push it through the open slit on your chain. Keep going until your chain is the length you want. (About 5 daisies make a bracelet; 10 make a crown—but it depends on the size of your daisies.)

- To complete your loop, use your fingernail to make your last slit larger—usually about 1 inch.

- Then, carefully push the first daisy head, the one at the top of your chain, through the larger slit.

267 HOW TO
MAKE A FLOWER CHANGE COLOR

Cutting board and knife

2 small glass jars (that can be recycled)

Food coloring

White flower (carnations and daisies work well)

- With the help of an adult, use the knife to trim a few inches off the end of the stem.

- Cut the other direction, and split the stem in half about halfway up.

- Fill both jars ⅓ full of water.

- Add 4–8 drops of a different color of food coloring to each jar.

- Place the flower so one half of the stem is in each jar. (If necessary, go back and split the stem a little higher so that the flower stays in the jars.)

- Wait a few days, and watch what happens.

268 HOW TO
PRESS A FLOWER

Pressing flowers is a great way to preserve them and make them ready for art projects.

Large piece of wax paper

1 or more flowers (to start, chose types that are a flat shape, like a daisy, and not a round shape, like a rose)

3 or more hardcover books

You can press leaves, too!

- Fold the wax paper in half and then open it back up.

- Place the flowers on one side, and close the wax paper with the flowers inside.

- Place the hardcover books in a stack on top of the wax paper to weigh it down.

- Wait 1 week. Then check on the flowers. They should be dry and flat. If not, put the books back and wait another week.

It looks like MAGIC, but it's actually SCIENCE!

When a flower is planted and alive, it soaks up water through its roots. The water travels up the stem to reach the leaves and flowers—it's called capillary action. When you cut a flower, it continues to soak up water through the stem.

MAKE A TOY PARACHUTE

Empty and clean plastic shopping bag
(or trash bag)

Napkin

Permanent marker

Scissors

Yarn or thick string

Small plastic toy

Tape

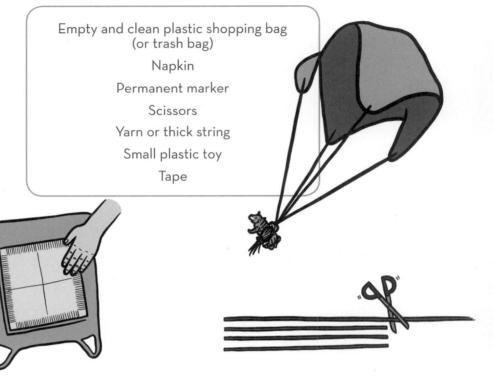

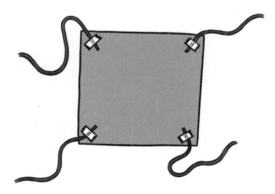

Smooth out the plastic bag. Unfold the napkin, lay it on top, and trace around the edges with the permanent marker. Cut out the square from the plastic bag.

Cut a piece of yarn about as long as your lower arm—from your elbow to your fingers. Cut three more pieces the same size so you have four equal pieces of yarn.

Tape the end of one piece of yarn to a corner of the plastic square. Repeat for each corner. Tie all 4 pieces of yarn in a knot a few inches from the bottom of the string.

Use the ends of the string below the knot to attach your toy. Take the parachute to a high place and let it fly.

MAKE A TOY BOOMERANG

A boomerang is a curved piece of material, usually wood, designed to be thrown into the air so that it turns and *flies back*. Boomerangs were originally used as hunting tools by aboriginal peoples in Australia.

Sheet of paper

Drawing tools
(colored pencils/pens,
markers, or crayons)

Scissors

Thin cardboard
(like from a cereal box)

- Trace the outline of the boomerang shape onto a sheet of paper.

- Cut it out. Use this as a template to trace the shape onto the cardboard.

- Cut the boomerang out of the cardboard, and decorate it.

- Gently tip and bend the edges that are shaded in blue until they stay bent up. These angles are for a right-handed boomerang. For a left-handed thrower, flip the angles to the opposite sides.

- Practice throwing your boomerang.

A boomerang is not a Frisbee.

Hold it on the star with the R. If you are left-handed, hold it on the opposite side.

Hold it vertically over your shoulder.

Snap it forward, and release it quickly.

★R

Some boomerangs need little adjustments: Tip and bend your edges a little more. Or bend each wing up slightly.

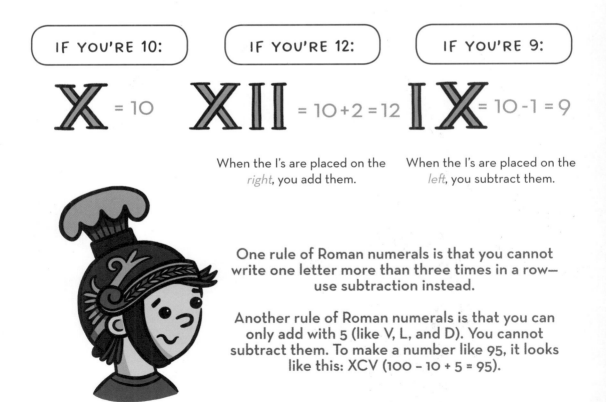

271 HOW TO
WRITE YOUR AGE LIKE AN ANCIENT ROMAN

Roman numerals are a system of writing numbers with combinations of letters from the Latin alphabet. It has been around for almost 3,000 years.

I	V	X	L	C	D	M
1	5	10	50	100	500	1,000

Start with the number closest to your age. Then use the letter I (which stands for 1) to add or subtract from the number until it equals your age, like this:

IF YOU'RE 10:

X = 10

IF YOU'RE 12:

XII = 10 + 2 = 12

When the I's are placed on the *right*, you add them.

IF YOU'RE 9:

IX = 10 − 1 = 9

When the I's are placed on the *left*, you subtract them.

One rule of Roman numerals is that you cannot write one letter more than three times in a row—use subtraction instead.

Another rule of Roman numerals is that you can only add with 5 (like V, L, and D). You cannot subtract them. To make a number like 95, it looks like this: XCV (100 − 10 + 5 = 95).

DRAW LIKE MICHELANGELO

More than 500 years ago, Michelangelo painted the ceiling of the Sistine Chapel over his head. Give this upside-down method a go!

Table

Tape

Sheet of paper
(the larger the better)

Drawing tools
(colored pencils/pens,
markers, or crayons)

- Crawl under a table with your materials.

- Tape the paper to the bottom of the table.

- Look up, and draw! (Michelangelo painted more than 300 characters in his artwork.)

- When you are finished, display your artwork on a ceiling— like over your bed.

DECODE A CAESAR CODE

- Write the alphabet *in one line* across the top of one sheet of paper. Then repeat this on a second sheet of paper. Line them up, one underneath the other.

- Choose a number, like 2. Shift the bottom paper two letters to the right.

- The two letters that fall off the end on the right should be brought around to the beginning on the left, like this:

2 sheets of paper

Writing tools
(pencils, pens, markers,
or crayons)

ABCDEFGHIJKLMNOPQRSTUVWXYZ
YZABCDEFGHIJKLMNOPQRSTUVWX

- Use pairs of stacked letters to code and decode a message, like this:

  - PICKLE
  - Code: NGAIJC

Can you decode *this* message?
(Check out page 201 for a hint!)

G JMTC KYPQFKYJJMUQ

In a Caesar code, you can shift the alphabet by 2, 5, 11, or *any* number. (Just tell the person decoding the message the secret number to use.)

HOW TO

MAKE A SMILING SANDWICH

Leave your sandwich open face, and it can smile at you.

> Slice of bread
>
> Plate
>
> Optional toppings:
> Meat—cold cuts, pepperoni, a hot dog,
> or sausage slices
>
> Cheese—slices, cubes, or strings
>
> Fruits and veggies—lettuce or slices of
> avocado, cucumbers, peppers, tomatoes,
> or other favorites
>
> Spreads—ketchup, mustard, mayonnaise,
> cream cheese, hummus, or nut butter
>
> Others—slices of eggs, olives, seeds,
> or potato chips (!)

- Place a slice of
  bread on your plate.

- Place your toppings
  on the bread to
  create a face.

275 **HOW TO**

MAIL A HUG

- Place the paper on the floor, and lie down
  on top of it—make sure that your head and
  spread-out arms are on the paper.

- Ask another person to trace around you.

- Use the drawing tools to decorate your torso.
  (Include a message on the back about who it
  is *to* and *from*.)

- Fold it up, stick it in the envelope,
  seal it, stamp it, and mail it!

> Large paper, as wide as your arm
> span (or tape or glue several
> sheets together)
>
> Drawing tools (colored pencils/
> pens, markers, or crayons)
>
> Envelope
>
> Postage stamp

DRAW SILLY CHARACTERS WITH FRIENDS

Sheet of paper

Drawing tools (colored pencils/pens, markers, or crayons)

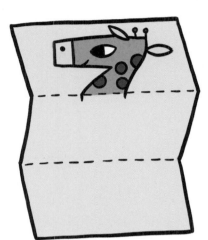

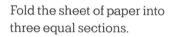

Fold the sheet of paper into three equal sections.

Have the first artist work on the top section of the paper, drawing a character's head.

Include necklines at the bottom of the section so the next artist knows where to start drawing.

Fold the paper to hide the drawing. The blank middle section should be on top. Have the second artist work on the middle section, drawing the character's torso, or middle parts. Include hip lines at the bottom of the section.

Fold the paper to hide the drawings. The blank bottom section should be on top. Have the third artist (or the first artist, if they are going again) work on the bottom section, drawing the character's legs and feet.

When the drawing is done, open it up to share.

277 HOW TO
MAKE AN APPLE STAR STAMP

Washed and dried apple

Cutting board and knife

Acrylic or poster paint and paintbrush

Small dish

Paper

- With the help of an adult, place the apple on its side on the cutting board. Cut it in half—one side should be the top, and one side should be the bottom.

- Find the star. Continue cutting until the star is on a small block of apple.

- Squeeze a glob of paint onto the small dish. Spread the paint out.

- Press your star stamp into the paint and then onto the paper.

What other fruits and vegetables can you stamp with?

278 HOW TO
COLLAGE A PAPER STAR

Pencil with an eraser

Sheet of construction paper (any color)

Recycled magazines, color newspapers, catalogs, photographs, or drawings

Scissors

Glue (bottle or stick)

- Draw a large star on the paper. Cut it out.

- Look through the recycled papers, and cut small scraps of different colors and patterns that you like. Place these in front of you in five piles, one for each color. Start with about 10 scraps for each color, and cut more if you run out.

- Choose a color for one point of the star. Take a paper scrap, and add glue. Place it on the star.

- Repeat with a new scrap. Continue until the star is complete, using a different color for each point.

MAKE A CELERY FLOWER STAMP

Cutting board and knife

Celery

Acrylic or poster paint and paintbrush

Small dish

Paper

- With the help of an adult, make one straight cut through the base of the heart of the celery.

- Squeeze a glob of paint onto the small dish.
- Take the cut edge of the celery, and press it down in the paint.
- Press the celery onto the paper.
- Use your fingers or a paintbrush to add stems and leaves to your flower.

Cut one rib of celery. Dip the bottom in the paint, and press it onto the paper. Some stalks make a heart shape.

195

280 HOW TO
PLAY GHOST

Almost spell words (without *actually* spelling words) to avoid becoming a GHOST.

- One player begins the game by saying a letter, any letter. For example: *S.*

- The second player repeats this letter and adds on a second letter. For example: *S-P.*

- The players continue taking turns, adding a letter each time. You must:

  - Add a letter that could be a word when more letters are added.

  - But not actually spell a complete word.

- If you spell a word, you lose the round and earn a *G,* the first letter of GHOST.

- If you add a letter that the other player doesn't think could later be a word, they can challenge you. For example:

  - If you add a letter to spell S-P-O-O, you can prove that it could be a word (SPOOK!), so you win—and the other player earns a letter of GHOST.

  - If you add a letter to spell S-P-O-B, and you can't prove that it could be a word, you lose and earn a letter of GHOST.

- The player who spells GHOST first loses the game.

281 HOW TO
PLAY THE NEVER-ENDING SENTENCE

These sentences go on and on . . . *almost* complete sentences without *actually* completing them to win.

- One player begins the game by saying a word, any word. For example: *The.*

- The second player repeats this word and adds on a second word. For example: *The cow.*

- The players continue taking turns, adding a word each time. You must:

  - Add a word that could be a sentence when more words are added.

  - But not actually complete a sentence.

- If you complete a sentence, you lose the round and earn a point.

- If you add a word that the other player doesn't think could later be a sentence, they can challenge you. For example:

  - If you add a word to say *The cow car*, you can prove that it could be a sentence (The cow car won!), so you win and earn a point.

  - If you add a word to say *The cow bananas*, and you can't prove that it could be a sentence, you lose and the other player earns a point.

- The player who earns 10 points first wins the game.

MAKE A PICTURE FRAME (FROM RICE!)

Small bowl or dish

Wax paper

Pencil

2 ounces of school glue (half of a 4-ounce bottle), plus more for the decorations

Food coloring

Spoon

½ cup of rice

Paper clip

Decorations—handful of colorful beads, glitter, or pom-poms

Photograph

Scissors

Piece of ribbon or string (about 1 foot long)

- Flip the bowl upside down onto the wax paper, and use a pencil to trace around it.

- Flip it over again, and squeeze the 2 ounces of school glue into the bowl. Add 6–7 drops of food coloring, and stir with the spoon.

- Pour in the rice, and stir again.

- Scoop the mixture out onto the wax paper circle.

- Use your spoon and fingers to form it into the shape of an *O*, leaving a large hole in the middle.

- Press a paper clip into the middle of the top of the frame until just a small loop is sticking out. Press down any rice mixture that comes loose.

- Let the frame dry overnight, then peel it off the wax paper. Flip it over so the back can dry. It may take 2–3 days for the frame to fully harden.

- Add glue to your decorations, and press them onto the top of the frame.

- Add glue to the back of the frame, and lay it on top of your photograph, framing what you want to see in the middle.

- After the frame has dried for a few hours, trim off the excess photograph.

- Tie the ribbon through the paper clip loop, and hang it.

283 HOW TO
MAKE A PAPER POUF

2 sheets of large tissue paper (or 8 sheets of small)

Scissors

Pipe cleaner, cut in half

- If the tissue paper is large, about 20 inches by 26 inches, stack both pieces. Cut in half vertically, then stack and cut in half horizontally until you have a stack of eight sheets about 10 inches by 13 inches.

- Hold both corners on one short side of the stack. Fold them over about 1 inch and crease the stack. (This tiny fold is now 16 sheets thick.)

- Flip the whole stack over. Hold both corners of the short side that is 16 sheets thick. Again, fold them over about 1 inch and crease the stack. (This tiny fold is now 24 sheets thick.)

- Continue flipping and folding until the entire stack is folded like an accordion. It will be about 1 inch wide.

- Wrap a pipe cleaner tightly around the middle.

- Use scissors to round each end of the stack.

- Slowly spread open the rounded edges on one side like a fan. Then spread them open on the other side.

- Then carefully peel and spread apart the layers until your pouf is a round shape.

Hang your pouf like a chandelier! String several poufs in a row to make a garland! Add a face to make a monster!

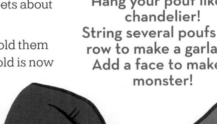

284 HOW TO
MAKE A PAPER POUF FLOWER

> Paper pouf
>
> Paper straw
>
> Piece of masking tape

- Find the pipe cleaner ends inside your pouf. Slowly and carefully push the paper away so that you can see it.

- Wrap both ends around the top of a paper straw.

- Wrap a piece of masking tape tightly around them to hold them in place.

285 HOW TO
MAKE A RAINBOW JAR

> Empty and clean glass jar or bottle
>
> Glue stick
>
> Scissors
>
> Balls of yarn in multiple colors

- Cover the outside of the jar in glue.

- Take a piece of yarn, and hold it with your finger where you want a stripe on the jar. Hold the inside of the jar with your other hand (so it won't get covered in glue).

- Wrap the yarn tightly around the jar as many times as you like: 3 times, 10 times, or 30 times.

- When you are done with this stripe, cut the string. Press the end into the glue on the jar.

- Repeat the steps with new colors until your jar is covered.

HAVE AN INDOOR PICNIC

Blanket

Optional: friends, family, stuffed animals, and real or pretend food

- Search for a perfect spot, and spread out the blanket. Picnic under a table, in your bedroom, or even in the bathtub!

- Invite friends or family, real or pretend.

  Stuffed animals and toys count, too.

- Serve food, real or pretend. Finger foods work well, like smiling sandwiches (page 192), soft pretzels (page 209), and cereal bars (page 37).

- End the picnic with a game, like two facts and a fib (page 112) or GHOST (page 196), or make up a secret handshake (page 29).

GO CAMPING IN YOUR LIVING ROOM

PACK YOUR GEAR.

(If you love it, bring it with you!) Grab a bag, and load it up with your favorite stuffed animals, toys, and games.

PITCH A TENT.

(A blanket tent that is!) Collect some sheets, blankets, and pillows to create a cozy place to play.

GATHER SOME GRUB.

(Picnic snacks for the win!) Make a bag of GORP. This is a trail mix usually made with granola, oats, raisins, and peanuts.

STARE AT THE STARS.

(Even if you have to make them yourself!) Add some string lights or glow-in-the-dark stars around your tent. Or cut some stars out of paper.

Use a flashlight to make shadow puppets on your tent walls— page 136 will give you some ideas!

288 HOW TO
MAKE A GIANT MARSHMALLOW

> Marshmallow
> Microwave-safe plate

- With the help of an adult, place a marshmallow on the plate and put it in the microwave.

- Cook it on high for 1 minute. Watch what happens through the window.

- When the microwave is done, carefully remove the plate and let the marshmallow cool before you touch or eat it.

289 HOW TO
MAKE S'MORES INDOORS

- With the help of an adult, preheat your oven to 375°F.

- Break each graham cracker in half. Place one half of each cracker on the baking tray.

- Place one piece of chocolate in the middle of each cracker.

- Place one marshmallow on top of each piece of chocolate.

- Put the pan in the oven for 3–6 minutes, until the marshmallows have started to melt—they should puff up larger and become lightly browned.

> 2 graham crackers
> Baking tray
> 2 small pieces of chocolate
> 2 large marshmallows

- Remove the pan from the oven. (The s'mores will be hot!) Place the other halves of the crackers on top, and push down to flatten the marshmallows.

- When the s'mores are cool, eat one and share one. Then, make s'more!

It looks like MAGIC, but it's actually SCIENCE!

Marshmallows are mainly made of sugar, water, and gelatin. There are lots of air bubbles inside, too. The heat of the microwave causes the water molecules to move back and forth, or vibrate, and turn into steam. The steam expands the air bubbles. The air bubbles expand even farther because they are also being heated. All this expanding makes the marshmallow puff up and grow larger.

MAKE A KUMIHIMO DISK

Kumihimo is both a method of braiding and a type of braid. To start, follow the instructions below to make a special tool, a kumihimo disk, which will help you form the braid.

Bowl, jar, or cup with about a 4-inch diameter opening or lid

Thin cardboard (like from a cereal box)

Pencil

Scissors

- Place the round shape on the cardboard, and trace a circle.
- Use scissors to cut it out.
- Draw a small circle in the middle a little larger than your finger. Cut it out with the help of an adult.
- Use your pencil to draw four marks on the circle: top, bottom, right, and left.

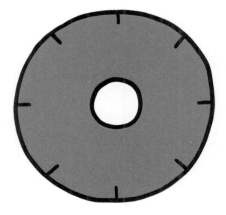

- Now draw 4 more marks, one in the middle of each of these.
- Last, draw 3 more lines spaced evenly between *each* mark. There should be 32 lines in all.
- Use the scissors to make a small cut on each line.

- To help with braiding, use your pencil to put a large dot between the top 2, bottom 2, right 2, and left 2 cuts.

Use drawing tools to decorate and personalize your disk, and keep it handy for making lots of braids.

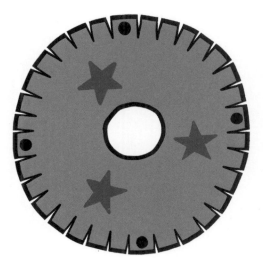

MAKE A KUMIHIMO BRAID

2 or more colors of satin
rattail cord or embroidery
floss (from 1-2 mm thick
works great)

Kumihimo disk
(buy one, or make your
own own—see page 202)

Tape

Scissors

- Cut four pieces of cord: Hold your arms wide in front of you, and make each piece about that length. (Using four different colors is a great way to learn the kumihimo braid.)

- Stack the four cords, and fold them in half. Tie a tight knot in the middle.

- Poke the middle of the cords through the middle hole of the disk toward the back. Tape them to the side for now. Then, on the front side, set the strings surrounding the four dots: two at the top, two at the bottom, and two at each side.

- Take the top cord on the right, and move it to the right of the bottom cords. Then take the bottom cord on the left, and move it to the left of the top cords.

- Turn the disk a quarter turn—so that the cords at the top move into your left hand.

- Repeat previous two steps over and over: Top right to bottom right, bottom left to top left, then turn to move the top to your left hand.

- After a few minutes, you'll start to see the pattern of the braid forming through the hole and extending out the back. (Remove the tape now as your braid grows.) Use your fingers to untangle the long strings under the disk as you work.

- When your braid is as long as you want (for a key chain, bracelet, or other use), tie several knots to securely end the braid.

MAKE SHADOW PUPPETS ON STICKS

Pencil

Cardboard or black construction paper

Scissors

A handful of wooden dowels (about 1 foot long), chopsticks, craft sticks, or paper straws

Tape

Optional: pipe cleaners

- Use your pencil to draw a small shape on the cardboard or paper. Draw anything you want a puppet of—a person, an animal, an object, a monster, or a place.

Trace a favorite toy.

Trace a cookie cutter.

Trace or draw favorite characters from a book.

Trace objects around your home, like a banana, toothbrush, or key chain.

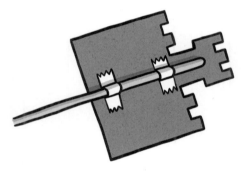

- Cut out your shape.
- Lay one wooden dowel on top. The shape should be at the top, with the wooden dowel sticking out the bottom. Tape it in place.
- Repeat to make more puppets.

Optional: Use pipe cleaners to add other shapes, like wings, on your puppets.

- Make a shadow puppet theater (see page 205), and put on a show.

BUILD A SHADOW PUPPET THEATER

Empty cereal box

Scissors

Wax paper

Tape

Drawing tools (colored pencils/pens, markers, or crayons)

Small lamp (like a desk lamp) or a flashlight

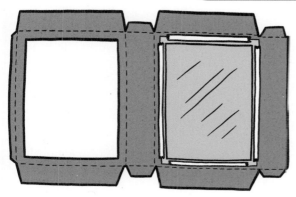

- Gently unfold the cereal box until it is flat.

- With the help of an adult, cut a large opening in the front and back. Leave approximately a 1-inch border on both sides.

- Cut a rectangle of wax paper that is large enough to cover the opening on the front of the box. Then cut two more the same size.

- Line up the three rectangles of wax paper, and tape them over the front opening.

- Fold and tape the box back together, but inside out. It should look the same size and shape as when you started, but the plain cardboard inside should now be on the outside.

- Use your drawing tools to decorate the cardboard.

- The side with the wax paper is the front—face this toward your audience. The side that is cut open is the back. Sit on that side. Place your lamp here with you, facing toward the front. (If you don't have a lamp, sit with your back toward a bright window.)

- Hold up your hands, small toys, or shadow puppets. The shadows will appear on the other side.

MAKE YOUR OWN TRIANGLE JUMPER GAME

Ball of air-dry clay (about the size of your fist)

1 marble or small round stone

Ruler

Pencil

- Flatten out the clay into the shape of a triangle. All three sides should be equal—at least 5 inches long and about ¾ inch thick.

- At the top of the triangle, press the marble down about halfway and then remove it, leaving a dent.

- Use the marble to make evenly spaced dents to complete the game, so that it goes, from the top: one, two, three, four, five.

- Use your pencil to carve your name into the back. Add patterns, shapes, or designs to customize your game. (If any cracks or sticky spots occur, dip your fingertip in water and smooth them out.)

- Follow the instructions on your clay packaging to let your game dry, about 2–3 days.

PLAY THE TRIANGLE JUMPER GAME

To win, plan your jumps just right and leave only one playing piece on the game board.

Triangle jumper game board

14 playing pieces that work with your board (marbles, pegs, etc.)

- Place 14 pieces on the board. One dent, any dent, will be empty.
- To play, jump one piece over another piece into the empty hole.

  YOU MUST JUMP IN A STRAIGHT LINE.

  YOU MUST JUMP OVER *ONLY* ONE OTHER PIECE.

  YOU MUST JUMP PIECES THAT ARE RIGHT NEXT TO EACH OTHER.

- Whichever piece you jump *over* is removed from the board.

- Keep jumping and removing pieces until there are no more pieces next to each other that can jump.

- To win the game, there must be only one piece remaining on the board.

MAKE AN ORIGAMI JUMPING FROG

Index card

Drawing tools (colored pencils/
pens, markers, or crayons)

Decorate one side of the index card. Flip it over.

Fold down the left top corner—it should match the right side of the card. Then fold the right top corner over to match the left side.

Unfold the index card.

Use both hands to push in the sides of the fold, like in the picture, and push down until the top is flat and creased.

Fold the left and right corners of this top triangle up to the top.

Fold in one long side of the lower part of the card. Then fold in the other side until they meet in the middle.

Fold the bottom of the card up to meet the very top.

Then fold it again halfway back down, and push firmly on the creases.

Flip the frog over, and push on the back legs!

297 HOW TO
MAKE CHOCOLATE SPRINKLE PRETZELS

- 2 cups of chocolate chips (or white chocolate chips)
- Microwave-safe bowl
- Spoon
- Parchment paper (or wax paper)
- 20–30 pretzels
- Sprinkles
- Airtight container
- Optional toppings: shredded coconut, crushed nuts, cookies, or candy canes

- Place the chocolate chips into the bowl, and microwave for 30 seconds on high. Stir.
- Repeat microwaving and stirring until the chocolate is melted. (This usually takes about 4 rounds, or 2 minutes. Stirring often will help prevent the chocolate from burning.)
- Tear off a piece of parchment paper about 2 feet long, and lay it on the countertop. Put the bowl of melted chocolate, pretzels, and sprinkles on the paper.
- Dip one pretzel into the chocolate. Let the extra chocolate drip off and then lay it on the paper.
- Add sprinkles immediately, before the chocolate hardens.
- Repeat with the remaining pretzels.
- Let the chocolate harden for about 20 minutes—then share and enjoy.
- Store the pretzels in an airtight container for up to 1 week.

298 HOW TO
MAKE BITE-SIZE CARAMEL APPLES

- Melon baller (or cutting board and knife)
- Apple
- Chopstick
- Handful of small pretzel sticks
- 10 soft caramel candies
- Microwave-safe bowl
- Spoon
- Optional: 1 spoonful of milk or cream

- Use the melon baller to scoop eight or more spheres from the apple. (Or use a knife to cut the apple into bite-size cubes.)
- Use the chopstick to make a hole in each apple.
- Push a pretzel into each hole, like a handle.
- Unwrap the caramels, and place them in the bowl. Add one spoonful of water (or milk or cream).
- With the help of an adult, microwave for 30 seconds on high and then stir. Repeat this about three times, until the caramels are melted and smooth. (Note: If the caramel seems too thick for dipping, stir in another spoonful of water, milk, or cream.)
- One at a time, dip the apples into the caramel. Let them cool, then share and enjoy.

BAKE SOFT PRETZELS

Baking tray

Nonstick cooking spray

2 packages of dry yeast (or about 2 spoonfuls)

2 bowls (1 large and 1 small)

Spoon

¾ cup of brown sugar

Salt

4 cups of flour

Dish towel

Egg

- Coat the baking tray with nonstick spray.

- Add the yeast to 1½ cups of warm water in the large bowl. Stir for a minute until the yeast dissolves.

- Add the brown sugar and ½ teaspoon of salt, and stir. Then add the flour, stirring as you go.

- Sprinkle a little flour onto the counter or table. Scoop the dough onto the floured surface, and knead it until smooth, about 5 minutes. (If the dough is still sticky, add a little more flour until you can knead it.)

- With the help of an adult, preheat the oven to 450°F.

- Cover the dough with a dish towel, and leave it to rise for about 15 minutes.

- Break off a piece of dough, about the size of your fist, and roll it into a long strip, like a snake. Shape it like a traditional pretzel (above) or however you like. Keep going until all the dough is rolled and shaped.

- In a small bowl, crack and beat one egg. Dip the pretzels into the egg one at a time, and let the extra egg drip off.

- Place the pretzels on the baking tray, and sprinkle each pretzel with a little bit of salt.

- Bake for 6–10 minutes, depending on the size of the pretzels, until golden brown. (For a crispy finish, broil for 2–3 more minutes.)

- Remove from the oven, and rest until cool enough to eat.

WEAVE A GOD'S EYE

A God's Eye is called an *Ojo de Dios* in Spanish. They have been made for hundreds of years.

> 2 wooden sticks of the same size (craft sticks, chopsticks, twigs, or even toothpicks)
>
> Balls of yarn in multiple colors

- Lay the two sticks on top of each other to create a cross.

- Take the end of one color of yarn, and hold it on the back of the cross.

- Wrap the yarn around the center of the cross like a figure 8 shape: Top to bottom, then right to left, about four times in each direction to help the sticks stay in place.

- Begin your weaving: Wrap around one stick one time. Then continue to the next stick and wrap around one time. Keep repeating, one stick after another.

- When you'd like to change colors, cut the yarn, leaving about 3 inches hanging off your weaving. Tie a knot combining the current color with the end of a new color of yarn.

- Continue weaving by wrapping once around the next stick. As you go, push the knot to the back, where you won't see it.

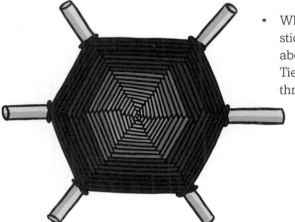

- When your weaving is almost out to the ends of the sticks, your God's Eye is done. Cut the yarn, leaving about 6 or more inches hanging off your weaving. Tie a knot to hold it tight. Then use the remaining thread to hang your design.

TIPS:
If the sticks are tricky to hold when you are getting started, glue them into a cross shape first.

Once you have the basic version down, add a *third* stick for a more intricate design.

301 HOW TO
WIN A STARING CONTEST

- Challenge a friend or family member to a staring contest.

- Sit face-to-face, and agree on the rules: Each person must stare straight into the other person's eyes. You win when the other person blinks, looks away, or laughs.

TIPS:

If your eyes start to hurt: *squint.*

Before your next contest, *practice* in a mirror.

Say your *funniest jokes* to make your opponent laugh.

If your opponent tries to make you laugh: *Think about something else,* like marshmallows, the ocean, or even your homework.

Before the contest begins, *close your eyes* to keep them moist.

302 HOW TO
DRAW A SILHOUETTE

A silhouette is the outline or shape of something. One way to draw a silhouette is with shadows.

Light source

Paper

Object to draw—you should be able to pick it up or hold it in your hand

Drawing tools (colored pencils/pens, markers, or crayons)

- To make a shadow, you'll need a light source: Use the sun (through a window or outdoors) or draw next to a lamp.

- Place the paper on a flat surface, like the table or floor. Move your object around, and experiment—where can the object be placed so that it makes a shadow on the paper?

- Use your drawing tools to trace the outline, then color in the silhouette.

303 HOW TO
BOWL WITH ANY BALL ④ ⑤ ⑥ ② ③ ①

6 targets (plastic cups or other objects that can be knocked over: plastic cones, used plastic bottles, toy figures, etc.)

Ball (any size and type)

Paper and pencil

- Set up your targets in a triangle shape, like in the picture.

- Walk about 10 steps away. Aim and roll the ball at the targets.

- Record 1 point for each target that you knock over, or 10 points for getting all of them in one roll.

- Play alone, with a partner, or challenge someone to a game: Who can get to 25 points first?

Play a miniature version on a table with a bouncy ball and small toy figures.

2+

304 HOW TO
PLAY OBSTACLE BALL

In this wild obstacle course, kick your ball the farthest to win!

- Begin this game outdoors. Players should move the objects around to create a course together.

1 large kicking ball for each player (like a soccer ball, rubber ball, beach ball, or similar)

Pile of natural objects or outdoor toys (pinecones, rocks, sticks, jump ropes, toy buckets, shoes, etc.)

SELECT A STARTING PLACE FOR THE BALLS.

MAKE OBSTACLES: TWO PINECONES TO SHOOT A BALL BETWEEN, A JUMP ROPE TO CROSS (OR GO AROUND WITHOUT THE BALL TOUCHING), A BUCKET TO TOUCH BUT NOT KNOCK OVER, AND MORE.

SELECT AN ENDING POINT FOR THE COURSE.

- The youngest player goes first. This player gets 10 kicks to see how far they can make it. (No hands allowed.)

- The other players each take their turns with 10 kicks.

- Whoever makes it farthest in the obstacle course wins.

Play again with more kicks: 15, 20, 30! Play again with a timer: See who can complete the course the fastest.

305 HOW TO
MAKE AN OBSTACLE COURSE

Objects of different sizes, colors, and shapes:

Indoors—pillows, scarves, bins, balls, masking tape, and more

Outdoors—Hula-Hoops, plastic cones, sticks, buckets, jump ropes, and more

- Begin your course indoors or outdoors: Select an object to touch as the starting point.

- Look at your objects, and make obstacles like those below—use your imagination.

SOMETHING TO GO OVER   SOMETHING TO GO UNDER

SOMETHING TO GO THROUGH

SOMETHING TO AVOID   SOMETHING TO BALANCE ON

SOMETHING TO MOVE

SOMETHING TO GO AROUND

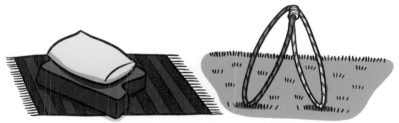

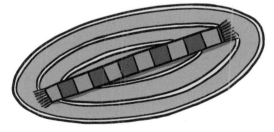

- Select an object to touch as your ending point. Ready, set, go!

Outdoors, add a sprinkler or hose!

DRAW AN OPTICAL ILLUSION

Drawing tools
(colored pencils/pens,
markers, or crayons)

Sheet of paper

Ruler

- Hold a pencil in your writing hand. Place your other hand flat in the middle of the sheet of paper.

- Trace around your hand.

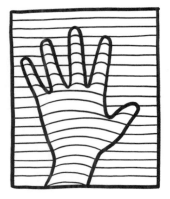

- Use the ruler to draw 10–20 lines across the paper, leaving the space inside your hand blank.

- Connect each line inside the hand with a curved line, like a hill.

- Color each stripe with one color that goes straight across the paper, including the curved lines in your hand.

DRAW WITH AN ERASER

Sheet of paper

Pencil with an eraser

Tissue

- Draw a large box on the paper.

- Use the side of the tip of your pencil to shade the entire box.

- Wipe the inside of the box with the tissue to smooth it out.

- Start drawing with your eraser. Erase areas to make lines, shapes, or even letters.

- Use your pencil to add back in dark areas to your drawing to finish it.

WRITE A REBUS

A rebus is a puzzle that uses pictures and letters to communicate a message, like this:

Can you solve this puzzle?

Here are some more ideas:

Now, write your own rebus message!

Answer Key (top to bottom): rebus, today, I love you, ice cream,
top secret, I ate blue cheese, swimming underwater, lunch box

309 HOW TO
PLAY SNAP

In this classic card game, win all the cards to win the game.

> 1 deck of cards for 2-4 players
> (or 2 decks for 5-8 players)

- Choose one player to be the dealer, and shuffle the cards. Deal out an equal amount to all the players, facedown.

- To start, the player to the left of the dealer flips over their top card and places it faceup to start a discard pile right next to their main deck.

- This continues left around the circle, with each player flipping over their top card and placing it to form their own discard pile.

- When a player flips over a new card that matches the rank of *any* other card visible at the top of a discard pile, *any* player can yell "Snap!" (A match could mean any two queens, or a 3 of hearts and a 3 of clubs, etc.) This player wins both *entire stacks* of discard piles. These are added facedown at the bottom of the matching player's main deck.

- If there is a tie and two players yell "Snap!" at the same time, things get interesting: Both stacks of discard piles are joined and placed faceup in the middle. When a player flips over a new card that matches this, any player can yell "Snap pool!" and win the pile. Play continues wherever it left off.

- Any player who yells "Snap!" by accident, when there is no match, must give one card from their main deck to every other player.

- When a player runs out of their deck, they can flip their discard pile over and keep playing. When a player is out of *any* cards, they are out of the game.

- The goal of the game is to win all the cards.

MAKE A SNAPPY DRAGON CARD

2 sheets of paper

Drawing tools (colored pencils/pens, markers, or crayons)

Scissors

Glue

Fold the paper in half. Draw a half of a dragon's head shape.

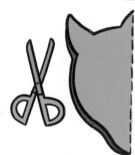

Cut out your dragon.

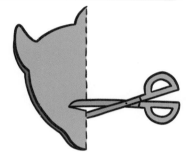

Make one cut on the fold, about half the length of your finger, around where the dragon's mouth should be.

Fold up both flaps. They should form a straight line across the top that is even with the fold line.

Unfold the flaps. Open up the dragon, and flip the mouth flaps inside out.

Fold the second sheet of paper in half. Add glue to the back sides of the dragon, making sure that no glue gets on the mouth folds.

Glue the dragon into the fold of the paper.

Use your drawing tools to decorate your snappy dragon.

311 HOW TO
STRING A POPCORN BIRD FEEDER

In colder months, animals' natural foods can be less available. Make a popcorn-and-fruit bird feeder for your local birds.

- Thread one piece of popcorn onto the wire. Leave it close to the end. Wrap the cut edge of the wire around the popcorn to create the bottom of your bird feeder.

- Pick up the other end, and thread on more popcorn. Add some fruits, too, if you like. Push them down against the bottom.

- Keep threading until the wire is nearly full. Then wrap the remaining cut edge around the last piece of popcorn to create the top of your bird feeder.

- Wrap your feeder around a tree branch, and watch the birds feast.

> Unsalted popcorn (Too much salt isn't healthy for birds.)
>
> Piece of thin floral or craft wire, about as tall as you
>
> Optional: cranberries (dried or frozen), raisins, or other dried fruit

312 HOW TO
FEED THE BIRDS

- Place the pinecone in the baking pan.
- Use the fork to spread the nut butter all over the pinecone. (This can get messy!)
- Pour the birdseed onto the pinecone one small handful at a time until it is fully covered.
- Tie the string around the top.
- Take the pinecone outdoors, and hang it from a tree.

> Pinecone
>
> Baking pan
>
> Fork
>
> Small dish of nut butter (or a nut-free alternative)
>
> Birdseed
>
> Piece of string about as long as your arm

MAKE A BIRDBATH

Recycled scrap paper, newspaper, or magazine

Plumber's adhesive (this is a waterproof glue found at most home improvement stores)

2 clean terra-cotta pots with saucers

Acrylic paint (1 or more colors)

Paintbrushes

Waterproof spray sealer

- Work on top of the scrap paper. Apply a thick line of plumber's adhesive around the top of one pot. Flip the other pot upside down, and press them together.

- Apply another line of plumber's adhesive to the bottom of the upper pot (which is now the top). Press one saucer down onto the adhesive.

- Flip the stack over. Apply a layer of plumber's adhesive to the bottom of the upper pot (which is now the top). Press the other saucer down onto the adhesive.

- Now your birdbath shape is ready. Paint it while you wait for the adhesive to dry.

- When the adhesive and paint are dry, move the birdbath outdoors. With the help of an adult, follow the instructions on the waterproof sealer to protect your birdbath. Allow the sealer to dry.

- Fill the top saucer with water, and wait for the birds to come.

314 HOW TO
JUMP BUTTONS INTO A CUP

Handful of buttons

Short cup

- On a flat surface, like a table or the floor, place one button a few inches away from the cup.

- With another button, press down in the middle of the flat button and slowly pull back. Watch the button fly.

- Keep practicing and you'll be able to aim and control the jumping a bit better. Play alone, with a partner, or challenge someone to a game: Who can get their button into the cup first?

315 HOW TO
MAKE A BUTTON BOUQUET

Turn buttons into a handful of flowers to give to someone you love.

Pencil

Construction paper

Scissors

9 buttons in various sizes and colors

3 pipe cleaners

- Draw a leaf about the size of your palm on the paper. Cut it out.

- Choose three buttons: small, medium, and large.

- Lay the leaf next to the largest button.

- Bend the end of a pipe cleaner so that it forms a long *J* shape. Thread the smallest button onto the pipe cleaner, and push it to the end, right before the bend.

- Thread the middle-size button onto the pipe cleaner and then thread the largest button beneath it.

- Poke a hole through the base of the leaf, and thread it last onto the pipe cleaner.

- Poke the end of the bend back through the small, medium, and large buttons. Wrap it around under the leaf.

Get more buttons and pipe cleaners to create more flowers for a bouquet.

316   HOW TO
PLAY NIM

Nim is a strategy game that has been played for thousands of years. It can be played with almost *any* number of *any* small objects. To win, plan your moves so that the other player picks up the last piece.

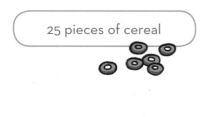

25 pieces of cereal

- Lay out three piles of cereal. There can be any number of cereal pieces in each pile. (For example, start with 4, 7, and 14.)

- The first player picks up any number of pieces they'd like. The only rule is that all the pieces must come from one pile. They can pick up just 1, some, or the entire pile.

- The second player goes next with the same rule. They can pick up from any pile they'd like: just 1, some, or the entire pile.

- Players continue taking turns picking up pieces. The goal of the game is to win by *not* picking up the very last piece.

317   HOW TO
PLAY GRUNDY'S GAME

2+

Grundy's game is a strategy game that is similar to nim. It can *also* be played with almost any number of any small objects. To win, plan your moves so that *you* divide the last pile.

10 coins

Play nim and Grundy's game again with different numbers of playing pieces. Or different objects: playing cards, paper clips, buttons, or even rocks or pinecones.

- Place the 10 coins in a pile.
- The first player divides the pile into two piles. The only rule is that the two new piles must have different numbers of coins: They can make 9/1 or 4/6—but they cannot make 5/5.

- The second player goes next with the same rule: They can divide *either pile* they'd like, but the two new piles must each have different numbers of coins.

- The players continue taking turns dividing the piles. The winner can always divide a pile. The game is over when one player cannot divide any of the piles—they all are down to only 1 or 2 coins.

It looks like MAGIC, but it's actually SCIENCE!

To turn cream and sugar into ice cream, you must freeze them until they harden. Ice alone isn't cold enough to do the job. But *salt* does the trick. Salt lowers the temperature at which water freezes—it lowers the temperature of the ice. This colder ice CAN freeze the ingredients and make ice cream.

318 HOW TO MAKE ICE CREAM IN A COFFEE CAN

> Recycled coffee can (empty and clean)
>
> Ice
>
> 6 tablespoons of rock salt
>
> Pint-size resealable plastic bag
>
> 1 cup of heavy cream
>
> 2 tablespoons of sugar

- Fill the coffee can halfway with ice, and add the rock salt. Put the lid on the can, and shake it.

- With the help of another person, pour the heavy cream and sugar into the small plastic bag. Seal the bag tightly, and double-check that it is fully sealed.

- Place the bag of cream into the coffee can, fully surrounded by ice. Put the lid on.

- Shake and roll the can for about 5–10 minutes. (If the can becomes too cold, wrap a clean towel around it or wear gloves.)

- Open the can and the bag: Has the cream frozen into a soft ice-cream texture? If not, reseal the bag, reclose the can, and shake for a few more minutes.

319 HOW TO

MAKE THE BEST ICE-CREAM SUNDAE

Have you ever made a real-deal ice-cream sundae?
Pile the ice cream and toppings high.

- Add one or more scoops of ice cream to your bowl.

- Add one sauce (or many).

- Add toppings.

- Share and enjoy!

> Ice cream and toppings
>
> Bowl and spoon

SAUCES

Chocolate sauce
Hot fudge
Butterscotch
Caramel
Peanut butter
(or a nut-free alternative)
Maple syrup
Berry jam
Honey
Cherry juice
Dollop of pudding
Scoop of applesauce

TOPPINGS

Sliced fruit
Berries
Bananas
Nuts
Peanut brittle
Popcorn
Crumbled cookies
Crumbled pretzels
Crumbled candy canes
Crumbled graham cracker
Shredded coconut
Pumpkin seeds
Sesame seeds

Dried seaweed
Sprinkles
Candy
Chocolate chips
Dried banana chips
Dried apple chips
Potato chips
Mini marshmallows
Cherries
Whipped cream
Cereal
Brownie bits
Granola

320 HOW TO

MAKE SNOW CREAM

> 1 can of sweetened condensed milk
> (12 ounces)
>
> Large mixing bowl full of clean snow
> (fresh snow is best)
>
> Spoon
>
> Smaller bowls for serving
>
> Optional flavorings: a spoonful of
> vanilla extract, chocolate syrup, maple
> syrup, sprinkles, or chocolate chips

- Pour the sweetened condensed milk into the snow until it is saturated, but not runny.

- Add any optional flavorings on top of the snow.

- Use the spoon to mix all the ingredients together.

- Scoop into smaller bowls for serving and sharing.

321 HOW TO

MAKE AN ART SCAVENGER HUNT

Make a scavenger hunt with an art-project surprise at the end.

> 2 large paper bags
> Writing and drawing tools
> Paper

- Select an art project, like How to Marble Paper with Shaving Cream (see page 225). Gather the materials, and hide them in one room or outdoor space. (Don't let other players peek!)

- Use pictures and words to make two lists of items to find:

LIST 1: SHAVING CREAM, BAKING PAN, PAPER AND SCRAP PAPER

LIST 2: PAINT, FORK, RULER

- Divide your players into two teams. Give each a bag and a list.

- Start the hunt: Tell both teams to fill their bags with the items on their lists as quickly as possible. Whichever team completes their list first wins.

- When both teams have completed the hunt, share your surprise: Now you have all the materials you need to make marble paper together!

> Make up your own scavenger hunt with the materials for any craft, recipe, or game!

MARBLE PAPER WITH SHAVING CREAM

Baking pan

Shaving cream

Paint (acrylic, tempera, liquid watercolor, food coloring, or a combination)

Fork

1 sheet of paper or more (any size or shape that fits inside the baking pan)

Ruler

Recycled scrap paper, newspaper, or magazine

For different effects, use different items besides the fork to move the paints around in the pan: paper straws, toothpicks, old combs, or even plastic toys.

- Fill the baking pan halfway with shaving cream.

- Add about 20 drops of paint on top. This can be a mixture of two or more colors.

- Use either end of the fork to gently swirl the colors in the shaving cream. (Go slow—if you swirl too much, you'll make the colors brown and muddy.)

- Lay a sheet of paper in the pan, and gently press it down.

- Lift it out, and lay it faceup on the scrap paper.

- Let it sit for a few minutes.

- Use the long, flat end of the ruler to drag across the paper, and remove the shaving cream.

- Set your paper somewhere flat to dry. (This may take over-night. Or dry it outdoors on a sunny day for faster results.)

- To marble more paper, use the pan as it is and add more colors. Or scoop out some of the shaving cream with the existing colors, and add more shaving cream for a fresh start.

DRAW IN 3D

HOW TO DRAW A
CYLINDER

① Draw a wide oval.

② Add two equal lines, like legs.

③ Connect them with a rounded line, like a smile.

HOW TO DRAW A
DIAMOND

①  Fold over the corner of a sheet of paper.

② 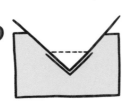 Trace the *V* shape of the folded corner in the middle of a different sheet of paper.

③  Inside the large *V*, draw one medium and one small *v*.

④  Connect the tops of the *V*s.

⑤  Then draw a "hat" by drawing two lines up from the middle *V*, with a straight line across the top.

⑥  Draw two lines up from the small *v*. Then draw boxes on the right and left to connect the largest *V* to the hat. Add a halo at the very top.

⑦  Draw two lines to connect the halo.

HOW TO DRAW A
CONE

① 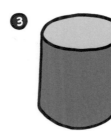 Draw a wide oval.

② Draw a line from each side down to meet in the middle.

Add a scoop (or more!) of ice cream to your cone.

324   HOW TO

DRAW A RECTANGULAR PRISM (AND WHAT LIVES INSIDE)

Drawing tools (colored pencils/
pens, markers, or crayons)

Sheet of paper

1

Draw a rectangle in the center of the paper.

2

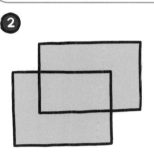

Draw a second rectangle of a matching size just up and to the right of the first one.

3

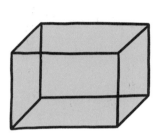

Connect each of the four corner lines.

MAKE IT A FISH AQUARIUM:

- Draw a fish in the middle.
- Fill the bottom of the tank with sand or gravel.
- Add plants, other underwater creatures, and bubbles.
- Fill the tank with water.

MAKE IT A HAMSTER CAGE:

- Draw a furry hamster in the middle.
- Fill the bottom of the cage with shredded paper, like confetti.
- Add a food bowl and water bottle.
- Add toys like a wheel or a ball.

MAKE IT A SPIDER TANK:

- Draw a spider in the middle. (Spiders have eight legs!)
- Fill the bottom of the tank with dirt.
- Add things for the spider to climb on or hide in, like rocks, branches, or logs.

MAKE BUTTER IN A JAR

Jar with a tight-fitting, screw-top lid
(like a Mason jar)

Heavy cream

Pinch of salt

Spoon

Medium bowl

Optional: paper towel and
parchment paper

- Fill the jar halfway with heavy cream. (For example: Fill a 2-cup Mason jar with 1 cup of cream.) Let it sit for about 30 minutes to come to room temperature.

- Add a pinch of salt.

- Put the lid on, and shake-shake-shake.

- After 4–7 minutes, you should hear clues that the cream has thickened into whipped cream. Keep shaking. After another few minutes, you should hear it get watery again, and there may be a sloshing sound from a lump moving around—this is the butter and buttermilk. You're close! Shake for about 1 more minute—usually about 7–10 minutes in all.

- Check your progress by dipping a spoon inside. Is it thick like butter? If not, keep shaking.

- When the butter is ready, pour out the buttermilk and use the spoon to scoop the remaining butter into a bowl.

- Fill the bowl up halfway with water and a few ice cubes. Knead and squish the butter into a ball—you are forcing more liquids out of the butter.

- Pour out the water, and replace with fresh. Keep kneading and squishing with fresh water until the water stays clear. (This should take a few minutes.)

- Squish the ball of butter tightly together—it's ready to share and enjoy. Or dry it with a paper towel, wrap it tightly in parchment paper, and store it in your refrigerator.

You've turned the liquid cream into a *solid* by separating the fats from the liquids.

326 HOW TO
SHAKE YOUR OWN WHIPPED CREAM

Jar with a tight-fitting, screw-top lid (like a Mason jar)

Heavy cream

Pinch of sugar

Spoon

You've turned the liquid cream into a *foam* by adding air bubbles!

- Fill the jar halfway with heavy cream. (For example: Fill a 2-cup Mason jar with 1 cup of cream.) Let it sit for about 30 minutes to come to room temperature.

- Add a pinch of sugar.

- Put the lid on, and shake–shake–shake.

- After 1–2 minutes, check your progress by taking off the lid and dipping a spoon inside. Is it thick like whipped cream? If not, keep shaking. (It often takes 4–7 minutes to get to whipped cream—but it's worth the wait!)

- -

327 HOW TO
POUR AIR

Large bucket of water (or full kitchen sink or bathtub)

2 clear cups

- Hold a cup in one of your hands under water until it is **full of water**. Turn it upside down (still underwater).

- Hold the other cup in your other hand. Turn it upside down *above* the water. Then put it straight down into the water so that it remains **full of air**.

- Hold the cup that is full of air just under the other. Tip it very slowly, and watch the air bubbles "pour" up into the other cup.

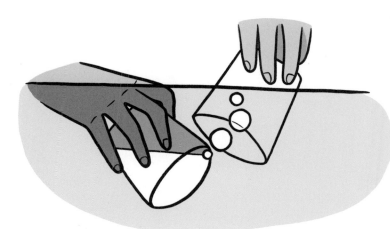

FOLD A PAPER BALLOON

Square sheet of paper (see page 8)

Fold the paper in half, and crease it. Open it back up.

Fold it in half the other way and then on both diagonals, opening after each fold, until the paper looks like this:

Using the folds, push in two sides to form a triangle, like this:

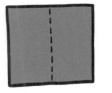

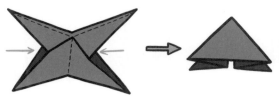

Fold both bottom corners up to the middle. Flip it over, and do the same thing on the back.

Fold both side corners into the middle. Flip it over, and do the same thing on the back.

FLIP

FLIP

Fold the left top of a triangle out, then in on itself, like this:

Tuck the triangle into the paper pocket just in front of it!

Repeat the previous two steps with the other three top triangles.

FLIP

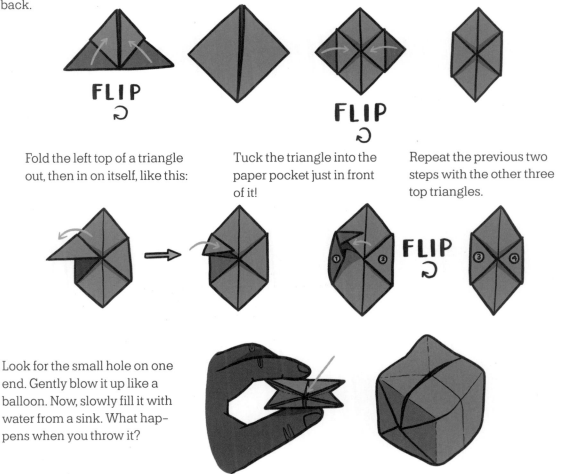

Look for the small hole on one end. Gently blow it up like a balloon. Now, slowly fill it with water from a sink. What happens when you throw it?

BUILD A BALLOON ROCKET

Ball of string (it must be thin, like yarn or kitchen twine, so that it fits through the straw)

Scissors

Paper straw

2 chairs

Balloon (regular round shape or long cylinder shape)

Binder clip

Tape

- Cut a piece of string about 12 feet long. (You could roughly measure from your head to your toes about three times.)

- Cut the straw in half.

- Push the string through the straw until the straw is in the middle.

- Tie one end of the string to the top of a chair. Tie the other end to the top of another chair. Move the chairs slowly apart until the string is tight.

- Blow up the balloon. Do not tie it shut—attach the binder clip so that no air escapes.

- Tear off two small pieces of tape, and attach the side of the balloon to the straw. (Look at the picture to see how the balloon is on its side, with the clipped end at the back.)

- Pull the binder clip (and balloon and attached straw) slowly toward one chair. (The binder clip needs to face the chair, with the front of the "rocket" set to shoot out across the string.)

- Remove the binder clip, and watch it fly.

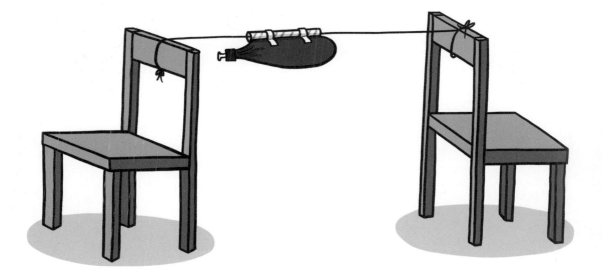

MAKE A PIÑATA

Bowl

1 cup of flour

Spoon

Scissors

10 or more sheets of newspaper

Ruler

Blown-up balloon

Piece of string about as tall as you

Decoration options: glue, small squares of crepe paper, tissue paper, felt, colorful paper scraps, cotton balls, feathers, or stickers

- Make papier-mâché: In the bowl, pour 1 cup of flour and 1 cup of warm water and mix with a spoon.

- Cut strips from half of the sheets of newspaper, each about 1–2 inches in width. (Cut more later if needed.)

- Set up a place to work—this will be messy! Lay out one full sheet of newspaper, and place the balloon on top.

- Take one strip of newspaper, and soak it in the papier-mâché. Lift it out, and rub off the extra goop with your fingers.

- Place it in the middle of the balloon, pressing down until it is flat.

- Repeat the previous 2 steps, with each new strip overlapping the strip before it a little bit. Leave an opening near the top a little smaller than your palm. This can be used to fill the piñata. Continue until the *entire* balloon has been covered 3–4 times.

- Let the balloon dry overnight.

- With the help of an adult, press your scissors into the top of the balloon (you may hear a pop!). Make two small holes alongside the opening. Thread a string through the holes to hang the piñata.

- If you'd like, glue decorations onto the outside. Then fill your piñata with candy or small toys, hang it, and take turns swinging at it with a plastic bat or broomstick until it bursts!

MAKE TIN CAN STILTS

Hammer and nail

2 empty and clean tin cans of the same size (larger cans work best: coffee, tomato, soup, beans, etc.)

Thick string or rope

Scissors

Optional: stickers or paint and paintbrush

- With the help of an adult, use the hammer to tap the nail into the bottom of each can to make a hole. Pull the nail out. Make four holes in all, two in each can, like in the picture below.

- Measure and cut a piece of string as tall as you are. Cut a second string the same length.

- Start with one string and one can: Push one end of the string through one hole and the other end of the string through the other hole. (If your holes are not large enough, widen them by using a larger nail or by using the same nail to make additional holes right next to your current ones until they become larger.)

- Use your hand to pull the strings out the open side of the can (being careful of any sharp edges).

- Tie the two strings tightly together with a few knots.

- Do the same thing with the second string and second can.

- Put on a pair of shoes, and stand with one foot on each can. Pull the right string up to your right hand and the left string up to your left hand. Pull up on one string to take a step. Let's go!

Decorate your cans with stickers or paint.

DO A ROUNDHOUSE KICK

①

Stand evenly on both feet, sideways to your target—your kicking leg should be in back and your other leg in front.

②

Bend your arms, and bring your fists up by your chin. Bring your kicking knee forward strongly and quickly, as if you were going to hit your target with your knee.

③

Let the turning motion of your body pivot the heel on the ground toward your target to strengthen your kick. Lean back to stay in balance.

④

Continue pivoting your heel a little more, while you lean back a little farther. Extend your kicking leg all the way—point your toes and kick your target with your shin.

Bring your kicking leg back, and return to your starting stance.

333 HOW TO
MAKE A SODA BOTTLE ERUPT

> 2-liter bottle of diet soda
> 4 scotch mints candies

- Take the soda and scotch mints outdoors to an area that is safe to get covered in soda.
- Take the lid off the soda, and set the bottle on a hard surface.
- Move quickly: Drop the four scotch mints into the top of the soda bottle. Then run away!

334 HOW TO
MAKE A CEREAL SLINGSHOT

> Scissors
> Balloon
> Empty roll of clear tape
> Electrical tape
> Handful of cereal

1 Cut a balloon in half. Throw away the end you'd usually blow through.

2 Pinch the tongs on the back of the empty tape roll to pop out the round spool.

3 With the help of a partner, use tape to attach the balloon to the spool. Place the cut edge of the balloon on the spool, and tape around it so the tape is half on the balloon and half on the spool.

4 Drop a piece of cereal through the spool and into the balloon. With your other hand, grab the cereal (inside the balloon) and pull it back. Let it fly!

235

335 HOW TO
MAKE FOSSIL COOKIES

Premade sugar cookie dough

Baking tray

Nonstick cooking spray

Small natural items (like cleaned shells) or plastic toys (dinosaurs, animals, or insects)

- Follow the instructions on the premade cookie dough to form individual cookies, and place them spaced out on a baking tray, sprayed with nonstick spray.

- Use your toys or natural items to press into each cookie to make an impression.

- With the help of an adult, bake the fossil cookies according to the instructions.

336 HOW TO
MAKE CARAMEL APPLE NACHOS

Cutting board and knife

2 apples

Large plate

20 soft caramel candies

Microwave-safe bowl

Spoon

Optional toppings: sprinkles, chocolate chips, chocolate sauce, sprinkles, cinnamon, crushed graham crackers, mini marshmallows

- Cut the apples into eight or more slices each, and spread them out on your plate.

- Unwrap the caramels, and place them in the bowl. Add 3 spoonfuls of water.

- With the help of an adult, microwave the caramels on high for 30 seconds and then stir. Repeat this about three times, until the caramels are melted and smooth. (Note: If the caramel seems too thick to pour, stir in 2 additional spoonfuls of water.)

- Drizzle the caramel over the apples.

- Add toppings to the nachos—then share and enjoy!

337 HOW TO
MAKE AN OCTOPUS HOT DOG

Uncooked hot dog
Cutting board and knife
Toothpick
Ketchup (or mustard)

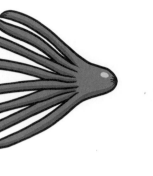

- Lay the hot dog on the cutting board, and hold the top. With the help of an adult, use the knife to cut down the middle of the rest of the hot dog.

- Turn it a little, and repeat this step so that the bottom ⅔ or so of the hot dog has been cut into four equal strips.

- Use the knife to cut each strip in half, forming eight legs.

- Cook the hot dog according to the instructions on the package.

- Use the toothpick and ketchup to add a face on your octopus.

338 HOW TO
HOST A CANDY CRANE COMPETITION

Crane candies to your mouth—and eat them first!

2 paper straws for each player

2 pieces of string for each player (each measured from your knees to your ears)

Pile of small candies or cereal

- Each player begins by laying their two straws side by side in front of them on a table. Tie one string around one end of the straws, and knot it, joining the straws together. Then tie the other string around the other ends.

- Lay 3 pieces of candy on top of the straws.

- Carefully hold the free ends of your strings, and loop them around your ears. *(Yes—your ears!)*

- Together count: "1, 2, 3, go!" Each player must pull their strings to lift their candy crane closer to their mouths. Eat all the candies to win!

Compete again with *more* candies on the cranes!

2+

PLAY RAINY DAY HOPSCOTCH

Play anywhere indoors with space to move around. Be the first player to get to number 10.

> Masking tape
> Small stuffed animal

- Tear off pieces of masking tape to create a hopscotch board on the floor.

- Use tape to write the numbers 1–10 inside the boxes.

- To play, stand behind the number 1 and toss the stuffed animal into box 1.

- Then hop on one foot to the first open box, 2. Keep hopping on one foot until you get to the top. (On double boxes, like 4 and 5, do a double jump with one foot in each box.)

- Turn around and hop back. When you get to 1, stay on one foot and pick up the stuffed animal.

- If you are playing with others, pass the stuffed animal to the next player for their turn to toss to 1. When they are done, you can go again, tossing to box 2.

- If you fall over or hop outside the lines, your turn is over. You must repeat that number again on your next turn.

- To win, be the first player to get to 10!

PLAY A GAME WITH ONLY TAPE

To play, choose a spot indoors or outdoors with space to move around. Jump the longest pattern to win!

> Masking tape
> (or painter's tape)

Add more shapes! Lines, letters, and pictures work, too. Break the "only tape" rule and create obstacles with pillows and blankets indoors, or sticks and shadows outdoors.

- Use tape to outline four large shapes on the ground: a triangle, square, diamond, and hexagon. Each should be large enough and close enough to jump in and around.

- The first player starts any two-part pattern: Jump to triangle, jump to square.

- The next player must repeat these jumps and add one more to the pattern: triangle, square, diamond.

- Players continue taking turns in order, each repeating and then adding one jump to the growing pattern.

- When a player makes a wrong jump—they are out of the round. The last remaining player wins.

LIMBO DANCE

> Long stick or pole (a stick from a tree, a piece of wood, a broom handle, etc.)

- Place the stick horizontal at about the height of your shoulders. Either two players can hold it, one on each end, or one player can hold an end and rest the other on a chair, tree, or other object.

- The game begins when the remaining player or players go under the stick one at a time.

YOU MUST LEAN BACKWARD, NOT FORWARD.

YOU MUST NOT TOUCH OR BUMP THE POLE.

YOU MUST NOT TOUCH THE GROUND WITH ANYTHING OTHER THAN YOUR FEET.

- After each player has made it under, the stick is lowered for the next round.
- Keep going to see how low you can go.

The game is even more lively with music so that players can dance as they limbo!

342 HOW TO
PLAY I WENT TO MARKET

Use your memory to make it all the way through the alphabet.
Hint: Silly words can be easy to remember!

- To begin this classic memory game, the first person declares: "Today I went to the market and bought apples."
They can say *anything* that starts with the letter *A*. Like: artichokes, alligators, or anchovies.

- The next player continues by adding to the list: "Today I went to the market and bought apples and bread."

- The next player continues by adding: "Today I went to the market and bought apples, bread, and caterpillars."

- The game continues as players take turns and go through the alphabet to *Z*. If a player forgets a word, the next player takes a turn and tries to remember.

Make up your own versions, like:
"Today I went to the beach and saw . . ."
"Today I went to outer space and brought with me . . ."

343 HOW TO
MAKE BURRITO BITES

Muffin tin

Nonstick cooking spray

8 eggs

Mixing bowl

¼ cup of milk

Pinch of salt

Spoon

Cutting board and knife

3 large flour tortillas

Optional fillings: small pieces of spinach, bell pepper, onion, tomato, mushroom, other vegetables, or cooked meat like bacon, ham, or sausage

1 cup of shredded cheese

- With the help of an adult, preheat your oven to 350°F.

- Coat the muffin tin with nonstick spray.

- Crack all eight eggs into the bowl. Add the milk and salt. Stir until well combined.

- Cut each tortilla into quarters. Press one piece of tortilla into each of the 12 cups of the muffin tin.

- Divide whatever fillings you like among the tortilla cups until they are each about half full.

- Pour the egg mixture evenly into the 12 cups, and add the cheese on top.

- Cover the muffin tin with foil, and bake the burrito bites for 20 minutes.

- Remove the foil, and cook for 5 more minutes or until the eggs are cooked through.

MAKE YOUR OWN PICKLES

1 or more cucumbers (enough to fill the jar)

Cutting board and knife

2 cups basic vinegar (white, apple cider, or rice vinegar all work)

1 or more clean glass jars (that can be recycled)

1½ tablespoons of salt

1 tablespoon of sugar

2 cloves of garlic

Note: This recipe uses one 4-cup jar. Adjust the recipe up or down for larger or smaller jars.

- Wash and dry the cucumbers. If they have a thin covering of wax, peel them.

- With the help of an adult, cut them into shapes: spears, coins, or other slices. (The smaller the shapes, the faster they will soak up the liquid and taste like pickles.)

- Pour the vinegar into the jar. Add the salt and sugar.

- Put the lid on tightly, and shake until most of the salt and sugar have dissolved—they should be mixed in so that you no longer see them.

- Open the jar, and pack the cucumbers in.

- Peel the garlic cloves, and add them whole.

- Add water to fill the jar and then put the lid on tightly again.

- Place the jar in your refrigerator. After 2 days, the pickles are ready to taste.

- Refrigerated, the pickles will last for 2–3 weeks.

Start with cucumbers, but then use this quick pickling recipe with almost any vegetable—carrots, cauliflower, and radishes are delicious. Add spices, too—dill, peppercorns, mustard seeds, or even bright yellow turmeric.

HOW TO

PUSH A COIN
THROUGH A TABLE

2 coins of the
same type

- Sit at a table, and secretly place one coin on top of your left knee, hidden under the table.

- Place the other coin near the edge of the table in front of you.

- Welcome your audience: "Today I will push this coin right *through* the table! First, I have to find the soft spot. All tables have one." Knock on the table in various places. Pretend to listen carefully.

- After one of your knocks, say: "Aha! I found the soft spot." Holding the fingers of your right hand flat against the table, pretend to sweep your hand back to pick up the coin. Instead, secretly push it off the table and into your lap. Gather your hand up into a fist, pretending the coin is inside.

- Reach your left hand under the table, and pick up the secret coin from your knee.

- Announce your trick: "Now I will push this coin through the soft spot. 1, 2, 3!" While counting, take your empty right fist (with the pretend coin inside) and knock on the soft spot you selected. At the count of 3, quickly slap your open hand down on the table to prove that it's empty.

TIP: When your right hand slaps the table, use your left hand (hidden under the table) to tap the coin against the underside of the table at the exact same time. This clinking sound helps the trick seem even more real!

- Slowly pull your left hand up, and reveal the coin!

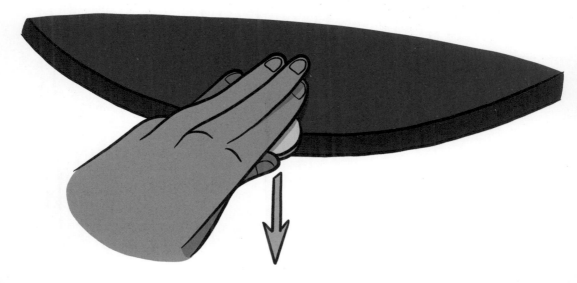

PLAY QUARTER CUP

Play this game indoors or outdoors on a hard surface—tables, wood floors, and pavement work well. Aim your coins into the cups to win points.

> Paper or plastic cup for each player
>
> Large handful of coins

- Have each player lay their cup on its side in front of them. The insides of the cups should face the other players—this is the goal.

- Divide the coins up evenly among the players.

- Have all the players sit the same distance from one another. Start at about 2 feet, and move farther as you get more practice.

- Count: "1, 2, 3, roll!" Each player starts with a coin standing upright, like a wheel. Aim at a cup, and give it a push! (Watch out for the cross fire!)

- Each coin that goes into another player's cup scores a point.

PLAY DINNER ROLL

A quarter and a fork are all you need for this dinnertime classic.

> Fork
> (make sure that a quarter fits between the tines)
>
> Handful of coins

- Lay the fork down upside down—this is the goal.

- Have all the players sit the same distance from the fork. Start at about 2 feet, and move farther as you get more practice.

- Take turns rolling one coin aimed at the fork. Start with the coin standing upright, like a wheel. Give it a push.

- Each coin that goes in between the tines of the fork scores a point.

MAKE LEMONADE

When life gives you lemons, keep them. Free lemons!!

> ½ cup sugar
> Jar with a lid
> 3-5 lemons
> Cutting board and knife
> Measuring cups
> Wooden spoon
> Pitcher

- With the help of an adult, pour ½ cup of water and ½ cup of sugar into your jar.
- Screw the lid on tightly, and shake, shake, shake (as hard as you can!) for 30 seconds. Check to make sure that the sugar has dissolved – it should be mixed in so that you no longer see it.
- With the help of an adult, juice the lemons:

    FIRST, ROLL EACH ONE AROUND ON THE COUNTER. THIS HELPS THE JUICES COME OUT.

    NEXT, CUT EACH ONE IN HALF.

    THEN SQUEEZE EACH HALF WITH YOUR HAND INTO A MEASURING CUP.

    SQUEEZE UNTIL YOU HAVE ¾ CUP OF JUICE.

    IF ANY SEEDS GET INTO THE JUICE, REMOVE THEM WITH THE SPOON.

- Pour the lemon juice into the pitcher. Add 3 cups of cold water.
- Add the sugar mixture a few spoonfuls at a time, and stir to combine. Stop and give the lemonade a taste. Add more sugar mixture until the sweetness is just right for you. (TIP: You probably won't need all of it!)

349 HOW TO
OPEN A LEMONADE STAND

Sheet of paper or poster board

Drawing tools (colored pencils/pens, markers, or crayons)

Table (or large empty box)

Lemonade

Paper cups

Help your lemonade stand grow: Hang more signs! Add decorations! Sell some snacks!

- Make a sign that announces your lemonade stand and the cost of each cup.

- Choose a location and spread the word. Pick a place that many people will be, perhaps your sidewalk or a park. Let people know about your lemonade stand by telling your family, friends, or neighbors.

- Set up on your table: Display your sign, and have your lemonade and cups ready to pour.

- When someone asks for a cup, pour the lemonade and offer it to them. Say, "I hope you enjoy the lemonade!" or "Thank you for buying my lemonade." Keep the money they give you in a safe place, like your pocket or a jar. (If you'd like, decide with your family on a charity where you'll donate the money you earn.)

350 HOW TO
FREEZE FANCY FRUIT CUBES

Fruit: lemons, oranges, limes, strawberries, cherries, blueberries, or raspberries all work well

Ice cube tray

Cutting board and knife

- Wash the fruit.

- If it is small, like a blueberry, place one piece in each section of the tray.

- If it is large, like a lemon, with the help of an adult, cut the fruit into pieces. Each piece should be small enough to fit inside one section of the tray with extra space around it.

- Cut up enough fruit so that each section of the tray has one piece.

- Fill the tray with water.

- Place it in your freezer until frozen (about 4 hours) or overnight.

- Pop out the ice cubes, and enjoy in a glass of water!

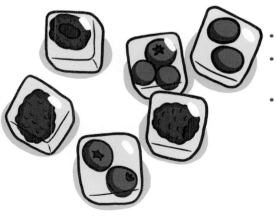

HOW TO
PLAY TELEPHONE

Transfer a message from player to player—listen close for unexpected changes!

- Gather all the players, and sit in a circle.

- Have the first player think of a short message, like: "Smelly shoes and socks are shocking." They whisper it one time to the second player.

  TIP: For extra laughs, say a silly sentence or tongue twister (see page 52).

- The second player whispers it once to the third player, then the third to the fourth, all the way around until everyone has had a turn.

- The last player then shares the message with the group: Did the words make it through the telephone the same as how they started? Or did they change?

In a larger group, divide into two teams. Whisper the same message to the first player on each team. Can either team transfer the message through all the players without any mistakes? Which team can do it the fastest?

352 **HOW TO**
WRITE YOUR OWN CIPHER

A cipher is a secret way of writing, like a code. An easy way to start is a substitution code—a picture, symbol, number, or even a color, replaces each letter.

One classic type of substitution code is called ROT-13. This stands for "rotate by 13 places." In this code, each letter in the alphabet is replaced with the letter that comes 13 places later, like this:

To say HELLO in ROT-13, you would write: URYYB

Make your own substitution code: Write the alphabet on a sheet of paper. Beneath each letter, add a picture, symbol, number, or color that you'll use instead.

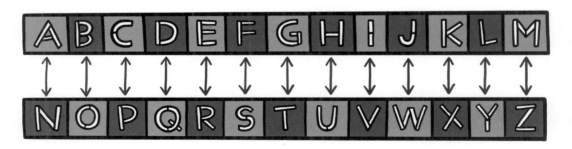

353 HOW TO
MAKE A PAPER CUP TELEPHONE

Did you know you can make a telephone from paper cups and string? Sound can travel through solid things like these *even better* than through the air. The sound vibrations travel along the string.

Toothpick

2 paper cups
(used and cleaned is fine)

10-foot piece of cotton string

- Use the toothpick to make a hole in the center of the bottom of each cup.

- Thread the string through each hole so that the ends are inside the cups. Then tie a very large knot in each cup.

- Hold one cup, and have a friend or family member hold the other. Move apart slowly until the string is tight. (This step is important: The sound vibrations will travel best if the string is pulled tight.) You can be in the same room, different rooms, or even outdoors.

- Hold the cup to your ear to listen, or hold the cup to your mouth to talk.

Experiment with a longer piece of string. How far apart can you stand and still hear each other?

MAKE A RAINBOW T-SHIRT

Empty cereal box (or other piece of cardboard)

Light-colored plain T-shirt

Permanent markers in several colors

Rubbing alcohol (70%)

Spray bottle

Practice your design by drawing on a paper towel. See what happens when you spray that with rubbing alcohol, too.

- Flatten the cereal box, and place it inside the T-shirt to make a hard surface to draw on. (This also will keep the colors from bleeding through to the back.)

- Use the permanent markers to draw shapes, lines, or designs on the T-shirt.

- With the help of an adult, pour the rubbing alcohol into the spray bottle.

- Spray the areas of the shirt with marker on them, and watch what happens.

- Wait for the shirt to dry and then remove the cardboard. Wash the shirt on its own so that the colors don't spread to other pieces of laundry.

MAKE COSMIC PAPER

Black paper (the thicker the better) cut to any size and shape that will fit in the bowl

Large bowl filled with about 2 inches of water

Clear nail polish

Recycled scrap paper, newspaper, or magazine

- Place a piece of black paper down in the bowl of water.

- Open the nail polish. Hold the brush over the water, and tap on the top to drop one or two drops of clear polish onto the water on top of the paper.

- Tip your head to watch the polish spread over the top of the water.

- Pick up the black paper from underwater. It will pick up some nail polish as you remove it. Place it on top of scrap paper to dry. In a few minutes, it will be ready.

Do this project with the help of an adult. Nail polish can have strong smells and should be handled carefully.

356 HOW TO
MAKE RAINBOW PARTY POPCORN

Baking tray

Parchment paper

6-8 cups of popped popcorn

1 cup of chocolate chips (or white chocolate chips)

Microwave-safe bowl

Spoon

Optional toppings: shredded coconut or crushed cookies, graham crackers, or candy canes

- Line the baking tray with parchment paper, and spread popcorn across it.

- Place the chocolate chips in the bowl, and microwave for 30 seconds on high. Stir.

- Repeat microwaving and stirring until the chocolate is melted. (This usually takes about 4 rounds, or 2 minutes. Stirring often will help prevent the chocolate from burning.)

- Spoon or pour the chocolate back and forth across the pan of popcorn.

- Add sprinkles (and any optional toppings) immediately, before the chocolate hardens.

- Place the pan in the refrigerator for 15–20 minutes. Share and enjoy.

357 HOW TO
MAKE RAINBOW FRUIT STICKS

3 or more types of fruit

Cutting board and knife

10 or more chopsticks (or other wooden food skewers with blunt ends)

- Wash and dry the fruit.

- Prepare the fruit: Peel and remove seeds if necessary. Then cut into bite-size pieces.

- Lay the fruit in rainbow order on the cutting board. Start with red (if you have it) at one end, through orange, yellow, green, and blue at the other end.

- Stack one piece of each fruit onto a stick in rainbow order. Share and enjoy.

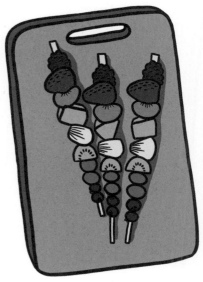

WRITE BACKWARD

If you write each letter, word, *and* line of a message backward, no one can read it. Unless they know the secret key . . . hold this page up to a mirror to read the message below.

2 or more sheets of paper
Pencil with an eraser
Mirror

- Write the alphabet on a sheet of paper. Flip it over, and trace each letter—now you have a backward letter guide.

ƧYXWVUTƧЯQ9ОИM⅃ꓘⱢIHϱꟻƎ◖Ɔ⸑A

- On a new sheet of paper, start your backward message: Begin at the top of the right-hand side. Write your first letter backward. (Look at your guide to study each letter.)
- Add the rest of the letters, each to the *left* of the last, to finish your first backward word.

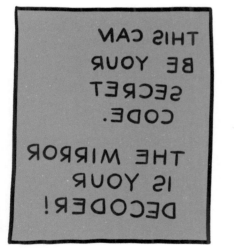

- Hold up the paper to the mirror to see if you can read it. If the letters are out of order, or not flipped, fix it.
- Leave a space and move to the left of your first word to add more words to your sentence. When the first line is done, drop down to the right-hand side of the next line. Keep going until your secret message is finished.

Some letters are the same backward and forward!

AHIMOTUVWXY

359 HOW TO
EAT AN OPPOSITES PICNIC

Set up a picnic blanket **under** your table.

Put your **food in a glass** and your **drink in a bowl**.

Or flip a plate over and put your food on the **bottom**.

Make a sandwich with bread on the **inside** and your favorite fillings on the **outside**.

Or eat **breakfast for dinner**.

Eat your dessert **first**.

Use your **opposite** hand to eat. (It's harder than you think!)

Have a conversation where **yes means no** and **no means yes**.

January 25 is National Opposite Day!

360 HOW TO
EAT A DOUGHNUT UPSIDE DOWN

Play indoors or outdoors—eat your hanging doughnut first to win. No hands allowed!

> 1 long string (12 feet or longer)
>
> 1 piece of string for each player (about 3 feet long)
>
> 1 doughnut for each player (any type with a hole, and without a filling)

- Tie the long string to secure it horizontally just over the head height of the players. It can be suspended between two trees or tied to furniture indoors.

- Tie one end of each player's string around their doughnut. Tie the other end to the longer string, hanging the doughnuts each at about the shoulder height of the player.

- Together count: "1, 2, 3, doughnut!" Players race to eat their doughnuts first to win—no hands allowed.

TIP: Eat from the bottom or your doughnut may fall to the ground—you'll lose the game *and* your doughnut.

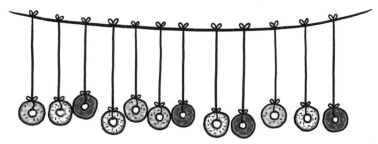

FOLD THE FASTEST PAPER AIRPLANE

Sheet of paper

Pencil or ruler

Long, wide wings are best for gliding far. Short, tight wings are best for speed.

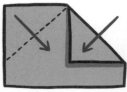

①

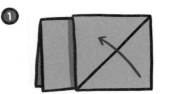

Fold the paper down to fold it in half. Then fold the bottom right corner up to meet the top fold.

②

Fold the bottom left corner up to meet the top fold.

③

Fold the top right corner down to the middle (the point of the triangle). Then fold the top left corner down to match. Press firmly to crease the folds.

④

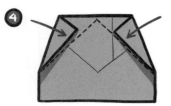

Unfold the two top corners. Then fold the top right corner in at an angle to match the crease line. Fold the top left corner in to match as well. (Look closely at the picture for this step.)

⑤

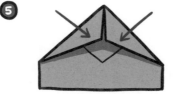

⑥

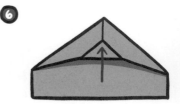

Fold the top right corner back down to meet the middle. Fold the top left down to match. Then fold the middle triangle flap up to lock them in place.

⑦ **FLIP**

Flip the airplane over. Fold it in half.

⑧

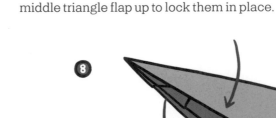

Fold both wings down. These are thick and tricky folds, so use an object (like a pencil or a ruler) to help you press down on them to get them flat.

HOST A PAPER AIRPLANE COMPETITION

Ready to see whose paper airplane is the best? Tear off a piece of masking tape, and make a starting line on the floor.

> Masking tape
> Paper airplanes (1 or more for each player)
> Measuring tape
> Sheet of paper
> Drawing tools (colored pencils/pens, markers, or crayons)

Test Flight #1: Distance

- Have each person start behind the line.
- Throw your paper airplanes, one at a time, as far as you can.
- Use the measuring tape to check how far each one flew.
- Record the scores.

Test Flight #2: Accuracy

- Place a sheet of paper about eight steps away from the starting line. This is your target. Have each person start behind the line.
- Throw your paper airplanes, one at a time, aiming at the target.
- Use the measuring tape to check how far each one was from the target. Bonus points for landing on the paper!
- Record the scores.

Test Flight #3: Height

- Select a target high on a wall—perhaps a window or the top of a shelf.
- Have each person start behind the line.
- Throw your paper airplanes, one at a time, aiming at the target.
- Record whose airplane flies high enough to hit the target.

Use your drawing tools to make a certificate for the winner.

363 HOW TO
MAKE A PAPER AIRPLANE LAUNCHER

Scissors

Empty cereal box (or other small piece of cardboard)

Ruler

Rubber band

Masking tape

Paper airplane

Pencil

Paper clip

- Cut a piece of cardboard about 2 inches by 4 inches.

- Fold it in half so that it forms two squares.

- Hang it on the rubber band and tape the bottoms together. Place more pieces of tape around the sides to keep the rubber band near the top. This is your launcher.

- To modify your paper airplane, bend the outer arm of a paper clip out, like this:

- Use the pencil to poke a hole in the fold near the front of your paper airplane.

- Poke the outer arm of the paper clip down through the hole, and tape it firmly in place.

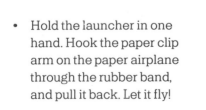

- Hold the launcher in one hand. Hook the paper clip arm on the paper airplane through the rubber band, and pull it back. Let it fly!

MAKE A PAPER AIRPLANE SUPER LAUNCHER

Chair

Handful of rubber bands

Paper airplane, modified with a paper clip (See page 254)

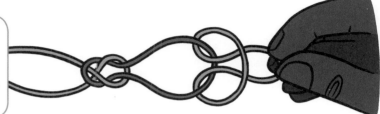

- Take your chair somewhere where it will be safe to fly—indoors or outdoors. Turn the chair upside down so that the back legs are sticking up.

- Loop one rubber band through another, and pull tightly.

- Continue adding rubber bands to your chain until it is just long enough to loop tightly across both back legs of the chair.

- Hook the paper clip (on your modified airplane) onto the rubber band. Pull back, and let it fly!

365 HOW TO
MAKE A THAUMATROPE

A thaumatrope is a simple toy that creates an optical illusion. A piece of paper has a different picture on each side. When the paper is spun quickly, the two pictures look like they become one.

- Drinking glass
- Index card (or sheet of thick paper)
- Drawing tools (colored pencils/pens, markers, or crayons)
- Scissors
- Hole punch
- 2 large rubber bands

- Tip the drinking glass upside down on the card, and trace around the circle with a pencil.

- Cut it out.

- Punch a hole on each side.

- Think of a picture with two parts. For example: a rocket and a blast. Or a fish and a tank.

- Draw *one half* of the picture on the front. Then flip the card over, **bottom to top**. Draw *the other half* of the picture on the back.

- Insert a rubber band in one hole. Loop it through itself, and pull it tight. Repeat on the other side.

- Hold one rubber band in each hand, and roll your fingers back and forth to spin the thaumatrope.

LET'S PLAY ALL DAY.